The carbon world

Planet Earth is a carbon-based world. All living creatures are made of molecules based on carbon atoms. It is strange to think that humans are based on carbon, the same element that diamond is made of, the hardest natural element in the world. Diamond is made only of carbon whilst humans are made of many other elements and molecules.

Why is a diamond so hard? The answer lies in its structure, the way the carbon atoms are arranged inside the diamond. Its tetrahedral structure is very strong – the diagram only shows a few of the millions of carbon atoms making up diamond). Atoms are very tiny particles and have never been seen – so how do we know how the carbon atoms are arranged in diamond?

Chemistry is a science based upon atoms – how they are constructed, how they are arranged in elements and molecules. and how they behave. The structure of diamonds was one of the first to be discovered by a technique called x-ray crystallography.

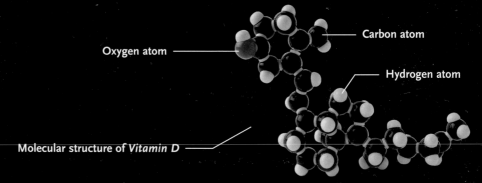

Oxygen atom

Carbon atom

Hydrogen atom

Molecular structure of *Vitamin D*

William Collins' dream of knowledge for all began with the publication of his first book
in 1819. A self-educated mill worker, he not only enriched millions of lives, but also founded a
flourishing publishing house.

Today, staying true to this spirit, Collins books are packed with inspiration, innovation
and practical expertise. They place you at the centre of a world of possibility and give you
exactly what you need to explore it.

Collins

DO MORE

Mixed Sources

Product group from well-managed
forests and other controlled sources
www.fsc.org Cert no. SW-COC-1806
© 1996 Forest Stewardship Council

Published by Collins
An imprint of HarperCollinsPublishers
77 – 85 Fulham Palace Road,
Hammersmith,
London W6 8JB

Browse the complete Collins Education catalogue at
www.collinseducation.com

©HarperCollinsPublishers Limited 2004

10 9 8 7 6 5 4

ISBN-13: 978-0-00-775549-3

Sam Goodman and Chris Sunley assert their moral right
to be identified as the authors of this work

British Library Cataloguing in Publication Data

A Catalogue record for this publication is available from the
British Library

Cover design by White-Card, London
Text page design by Sally Boothroyd
New artwork by Jerry Fowler
Printed and bound by Printing Express, Hong Kong

This high quality material is endorsed by Edexcel and has been
through a rigorous quality assurance programme to ensure that it
is a suitable companion to the specification for both learners and
teachers.
This does not mean that its contents will be used verbatim when
setting examinations nor is it to be read as being the official
specification – a copy of which is available at **www.edexcel.org.uk**

Acknowledgements:
The Authors and Publishers are grateful to the following for
permission to reproduce copyright material:

Edexcel Ltd: pp 151 – 163
Edexcel Ltd accept no responsibility whatsoever for the accuracy or
method of working in the answers given.

Photographs
Complete Weed Control Ltd 69; DeBeers 39; Lesley Garland Photo
Library 67; GeoScience Photos 109 (T); GSF Photo Library 34; Getty
Images 63, 130 (M); V Habbick Visions 29; Jupiterimages
Corporation © 2006 18, 134, 159 - 161; Andrew Lambert Photographs
9, 23, 26, 51, 52, 55, 57, 59, 60, 62, 72, 76, 79, 82, 89, 109 (B), 110,
124; Andrew McClenaghan 38 (B); Lawrence Migdale 27; Cordelia
Molloy 92; Alfred Pasieka 38 (T); Science Photo Library 19; S
Summerhays 68; David Vincent 4; South American Pictures 95; Tony
Waltham/Geophotos 130 (Tx3 & B)

Inside Front Cover spread: Diamond in rock – DK Images/ Harry
Taylor © Dorling Kindersley; Layer structure of graphite – DK
Images/ Andy Crawford, Tim Ridley © Dorling Kindersley; Vitamin D
– DK Images © Dorling Kindersley; Molecular structure of diamond
– DK Images/ Andy Crawford, Tim Ridley © Dorling Kindersley; Man
and woman – Getty Images/ Rubberball; Palm tree – Getty Images/
Jon Shireman

Section spreads: pp6/7 Whiteboard – Getty Images/ Ryan McVay;
Floating Atoms – Joerg Hartmannsgruber; pp48/49 Periodic table –
Joerg Hartmannsgruber; pp86/87 Refinery © Macduff
Everton/CORBIS; Distillation tower – Joerg Hartmannsgruber; pp
100/101 Wood-burning fire – Alexander Lowry/ Science photo Library;
Triangle Diagram – Joerg Hartmannsgruber; pp126/127 Hydrogen
Fuel cell – Daimler Chrysler AG © DaimlerChrysler AG

Every effort has been made to contact the holders of copyright
material, but if any have been inadvertently overlooked, the
Publishers will be pleased to make the necessary arrangements at
the first opportunity.

IGCSE

for Edexcel

CHEMISTRY

by Sam Goodman and Chris Sunley

WELLINGTON COLLEGE
CHEMISTRY DEPARTMENT

Name	House	School Number	Date
Andrew Veale (coch)	Raglan		done
Aidan Kirby	R.		

GETTING THE BEST FROM THE BOOK

Welcome to *IGCSE Chemistry for Edexcel*. This textbook and the accompanying CD-ROM have been designed to help you understand all of the requirements needed to succeed in the Edexcel IGCSE Chemistry course. Just as there are five sections in the Edexcel syllabus so there are five sections in the textbook: Principle of Chemistry, Chemistry of the Elements, Organic Chemistry, Physical Chemistry and Chemistry in Society. Each section in the book covers the essential knowledge and skills you need. The textbook also has some very useful features which have been designed to really help you understand all the aspects of Chemistry which you will need to know for this specification.

Coverage of each topic is linked closely to the Edexcel specification so that you build a powerful knowledge-base with which to succeed in the examination.

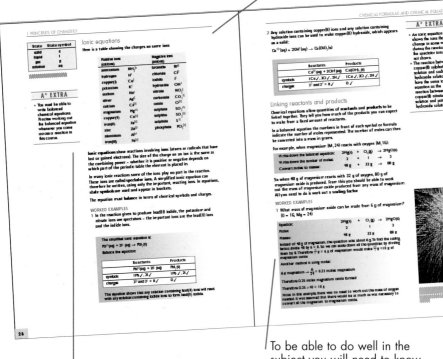

Photographic images really help in visualising the information you need.

This section has been designed to challenge those who want to achieve the very top grades. The A* extra feature is normally an extra piece of information or a tip.

To be able to do well in the subject you will need to know how to complete chemical calculations. The worked examples in the text take you through the question step-by-step to help you really understand.

There will be two stages to your assessment on the course because Edexcel IGCSE Chemistry is assessed in the following manner:

Paper 1 – Examination 1F – The Foundation Tier, worth 80% of the marks.

OR

Paper 2 – Examination 2H – The Higher Tier, worth 80% of the marks.

AND

Paper 3 – Examination 3 - common to both tiers, worth 20% of the marks

OR

Paper 4 – Coursework – common to both tiers, worth 20% of the marks.

Collins *IGCSE Chemistry for Edexcel* covers all of the topics and skills you will need to achieve success, whichever assessment pathway you are entered for.

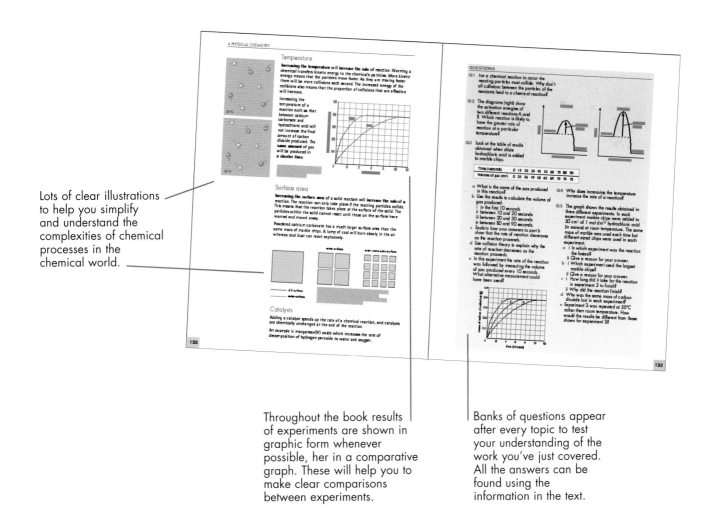

Lots of clear illustrations to help you simplify and understand the complexities of chemical processes in the chemical world.

Throughout the book results of experiments are shown in graphic form whenever possible, her in a comparative graph. These will help you to make clear comparisons between experiments.

Banks of questions appear after every topic to test your understanding of the work you've just covered. All the answers can be found using the information in the text.

IGCSE Chemistry CD-ROM

To help you through the course we have added this unique CD-ROM which may be able to be used in class or by yourself as part of your private study. To allow you to really understand the subject as you progress through the course we have added the following features to the CD-ROM:

LIST OF VIDEOS ON THE CHEMISTRY CD ROM
1. Safety
2. Hazards
3. Measuring liquids
4. Measuring mass
5. Time
6. Temperature
7. Chromatography
8. Filtration
9. Evaporation
10. Titration
11. Distillation
12. Identifying unknown compounds
13. Identifying gases
14. Flame tests
15. Identifying metals in solution
16. Identifying ammonium compounds
17. Identifying non-metals
18. Salts
19. Reduction and oxidation
20. Thermal decomposition

VIDEO FILMS

Chemistry is a practical subject and to reinforce your studies the CD-ROM has 20 short films which cover experiments and practical work. Each of the films covers an area which you need to know well for the practical section of the course. The information in the films will also help you with the knowledge required in other parts of the specification. You can use the films to help you understand the topic you are currently studying or perhaps come back to them when you want to revise for the exam.

Each of the films has sound too so if you are watching them in a library or quiet study area you may need headphones.

QUESTION BANK

"Practice makes perfect", so the saying goes, and we have included a large bank of questions related to the Chemistry specification to help you understand the topics you will be studying.

Just like the films your teacher may be able to use this in class or you may want to try the questions in your private study sessions.

These questions will reinforce the knowledge you have gained in the classroom and through using the textbook and could also be used when you are revising for your examinations. Don't try to do all the questions at once though; the most effective way to use this feature is by trying some of the questions every now and then to test yourself. In this way you will know where you need to do a little more work. The questions are not full 'exam-type' questions that you will be set by your IGCSE examiners. Some of the questions test underlying principles that are not specifically mentioned in your specification.

Good luck with your IGCSE Chemistry studies. This book and the CD-ROM provide you with stimulating, interesting and motivating learning resources that we are sure will help you succeed in your chemistry course.

OPERATING SYSTEMS REQUIRED AND SET-UP INSTRUCTIONS.

Mac System requirements
500 MHz PowerPC G3 and later
Mac OS X 10.1.x and above
128MB RAM
Microsoft Internet Explorer 5.2, Firefox 1.x, Mozilla 1.x, Netscape 7.x and above, Opera 6, or Safari 1.x and above (Mac OS X 10.2.x only)
325 MB of free hard disc space.

To run the program from the CD
1 Insert the CD into the drive
2 When the CD icon appears on the desktop, double-click it
3 Double-click Collins IGCSE Chemistry.html

To install the program to run from the hard drive
1 Insert the CD into the drive
2 When the CD icon appears on the desktop, double-click it to open a finder window
3 Drag Collins IGCSE Chemistry.html to the desktop
4 Drag Collins IGCSE Chemistry Content to the desktop.

PC System requirements
450 MHz Intel Pentium II processor (or equivalent) and later
Windows 98/ME/NT/2000/XP
128MB RAM
Microsoft Internet Explorer 5.5, Firefox 1.x, Mozilla 1.x, Netscape 7.x and above, Opera 7.11 and above
325 MB of hard disc space

To run the program from the CD
1 Insert the CD into the drive
2 Double-click on the CD-ROM drive icon inside My Computer
3 Double-click on Collins IGCSE Chemistry.html

To install the program to run from the hard drive
1 Insert the IGCSE Chemistry disc into your CD-ROM drive
2 Double-click on the CD-ROM drive icon inside My Computer
3 Double-click on the SETUP.EXE
4 Follow onscreen instructions. These include instructions concerning the Macromedia Flash Player included with and required by the program.
5 When the installation is complete, remove the CD from the drive.

For free technical support, call our helpline on: Tel.: + 44 141 306 3322 or send an email to: it.helpdesk@harpercollins.co.uk.

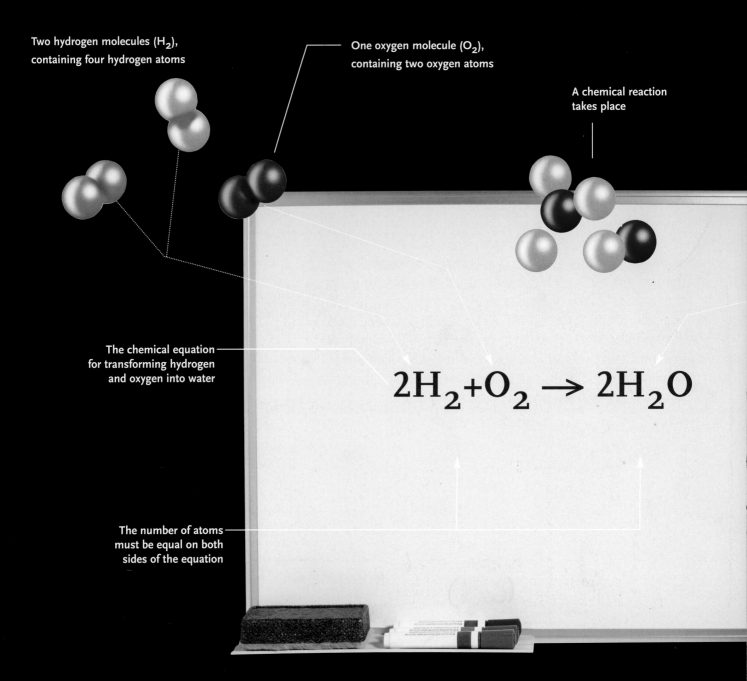

Two hydrogen molecules (H_2), containing four hydrogen atoms

One oxygen molecule (O_2), containing two oxygen atoms

A chemical reaction takes place

The chemical equation for transforming hydrogen and oxygen into water

$$2H_2 + O_2 \rightarrow 2H_2O$$

The number of atoms must be equal on both sides of the equation

A universal language

All over the world people use different languages to communicate. Chemistry has its own language. Every chemical element has a symbol, like O for oxygen; when writing you join letters together to make words; in chemistry you join element symbols together to make formulae.

A water molecule has two hydrogen atoms and one oxygen atom. The formula for water is H2O. Water is a 'compound'. When elements or compounds interact with each other to produce different substances this is called a chemical reaction.

To describe a chemical reaction we write an equation – equations are the 'sentences' of chemistry. The language of chemistry is universal, which means that scientists from Asia to the Americas, from the Arctic to the Antarctic, can understand the equations others have written.

Chapter 1

PRINCIPLES OF CHEMISTRY

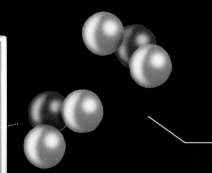

Two water molecules (H_2O)

Atoms

The kinetic theory of matter

The kinetic theory of matter is the idea that all matter, whether solid, liquid or gas, is made up of extremely tiny particles. The particles are moving all the time.

States of matter

HOW DO SOLIDS, LIQUIDS AND GASES DIFFER?

Almost all substances can be classified as solids, liquids or gases or as various mixtures of these three. These are described as the three states of matter, and they each have different properties, depending on how strongly the particles are held together.

- Solids have a fixed volume and shape.

- Liquids have a fixed volume but no definite shape. They take up the shape of the container in which they are held.

- Gases have no fixed volume or shape. They spread out to fill whatever container or space they are in.

Substances don't always exist in the same state - depending on the physical conditions they change from one state to another.

Some substances can exist in all three states in the natural world - a good example of this is water.

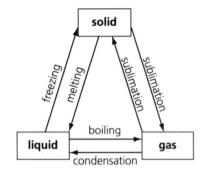

A substance can change from one state to another depending on the physical conditions.

Water covers nearly four-fifths of the Earth's surface. Here all three states of matter exist together – solid water (the ice) is floating in liquid water (the ocean) and the surrounding air contains water vapour (the clouds).

Matter can, in fact, exist in states other than the three descirbed here – for example plasma. Your teacher should be able to tell you more about this.

WHY DO SOLIDS, LIQUIDS AND GASES BEHAVE DIFFERENTLY?

The ways that solids, liquids and gases behave can be explained if we think of all matter as being made up of very small particles that are in constant motion. This idea has been summarised in the Kinetic Theory of Matter.

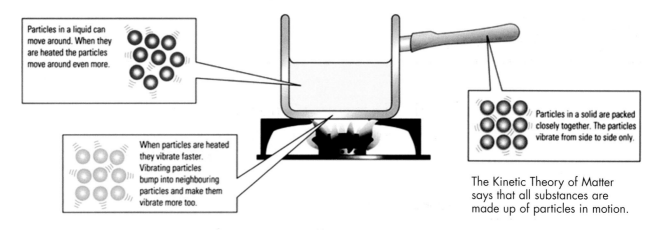

Particles in a liquid can move around. When they are heated the particles move around even more.

When particles are heated they vibrate faster. Vibrating particles bump into neighbouring particles and make them vibrate more too.

Particles in a solid are packed closely together. The particles vibrate from side to side only.

The Kinetic Theory of Matter says that all substances are made up of particles in motion.

Evidence for the kinetic theory

Scientists believe the kinetic theory because of the evidence from simple experiments.

DILUTION OF COLOURED SOLUTIONS

These photos show purple crystals of potassium manganate(VII) dissolving in water.

There are no water currents, so only the kinetic theory can explain this. The particles of the crystal gradually move into the water and mix with the water particles.

DIFFUSION EXPERIMENTS

These photos show a jar of air and a jar of bromine gas. Bromine vapour is red-brown and heavier than air.

After about 24 hours (right hand photo) the bromine vapour has spread out throughout both jars. This is known as **diffusion**. Kinetic theory says that the particles of bromine gas can move around randomly so that they can fill both gas jars. This also occurs with hydrogen and air.

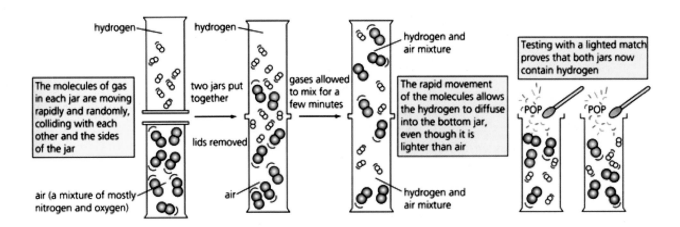

BROWNIAN MOTION

The Scottish scientist Robert Brown looked at pollen in water using a microscope. He saw that the pollen grains were always moving on the spot. Kinetic theory explains this by saying that the pollen grains are being pushed around by the tiny particles in the water that are always moving. You can see Brownian motion in a smoke cell. The smoke particles move about because they are constantly pushed around by the tiny moving particles of air.

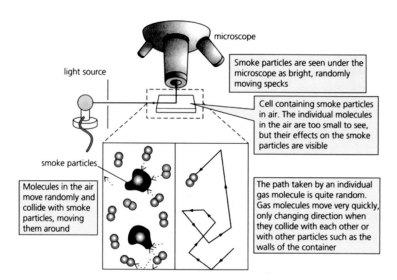

The **rate of diffusion** of a gas depends on its mass – molecules with a higher mass move more slowly than ones with a lower mass, as the experiment below shows.

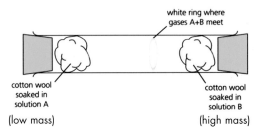

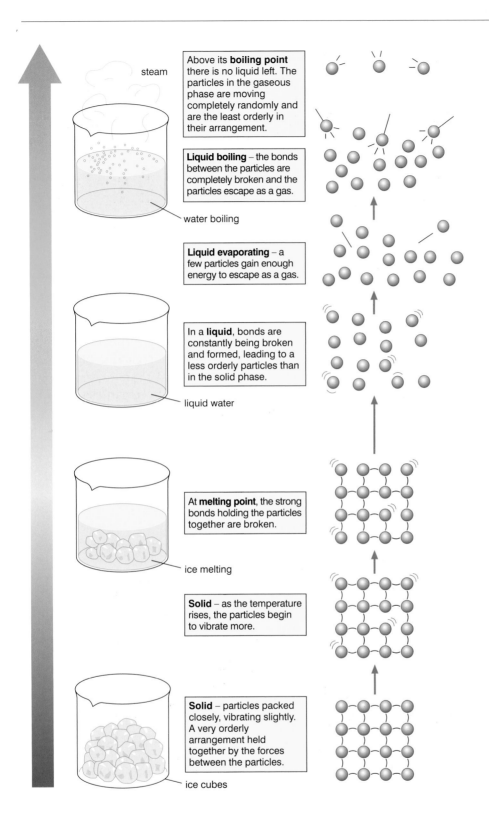

steam

Above its **boiling point** there is no liquid left. The particles in the gaseous phase are moving completely randomly and are the least orderly in their arrangement.

Liquid boiling – the bonds between the particles are completely broken and the particles escape as a gas.

water boiling

Liquid evaporating – a few particles gain enough energy to escape as a gas.

In a **liquid**, bonds are constantly being broken and formed, leading to a less orderly particles than in the solid phase.

liquid water

At **melting point**, the strong bonds holding the particles together are broken.

ice melting

Solid – as the temperature rises, the particles begin to vibrate more.

Solid – particles packed closely, vibrating slightly. A very orderly arrangement held together by the forces between the particles.

ice cubes

Elements and atoms

All matter is made from **elements**. Elements cannot be broken down into simpler substances. Elements are made up of only one kind of the same small particle. These small particles are called **atoms**. The atoms of an element contain the same number of protons and behave chemically the same.

Atomic mass and relative atomic mass

All the atoms of a given element have the same mass. The atoms of different elements have different masses.

Atoms are far too light to be weighed. Instead scientists have developed a **relative atomic mass** scale. Initially the hydrogen atom, the lightest atom, was chosen as the unit that all other atoms were weighed in terms of.

On this scale, a carbon atom weighs the same as 12 hydrogen atoms, so carbon's relative atomic mass was given as 12.

Using this relative mass scale you can see, for example, that:

- 1 atom of magnesium has 24 × the mass of 1 atom of hydrogen

- 1 atom of magnesium has 2 × the mass of 1 atom of carbon

- 1 atom of copper has 2 × the mass of 1 atom of sulphur

	Hydrogen	Carbon	Oxygen	Magnesium	Sulphur	Calcium	Copper
Symbol	H	C	O	Mg	S	Ca	Cu
Relative atomic mass	1	12	16	24	32	40	64

Recently, the reference point has been changed to carbon and the relative atomic mass is defined as:

the mass of an atom on a scale where the mass of a carbon atom is 12 units.

Relative atomic mass is written as A_r.

Moles of atoms and the Avogadro constant

The **mole** is a very large number, approximately 6×10^{23}.
That is 600 000 000 000 000 000 000 000.

6×10^{23} atoms of hydrogen have a mass of 1 g.

6×10^{23} atoms of carbon have a mass of 12 g.

6×10^{23} atoms of magnesium have a mass of 24 g.

32 g
Sulphur

56 g
Iron

64 g
Copper

So the relative atomic mass (A_r) of an element expressed in grams contains one mole of atoms. This means that the number of atoms of an element can be worked out by weighing.

These all contain 1 mole of atoms:

| 12 g | 24 g | 32 g | 56 g | 64 g |
| Carbon | Magnesium | Sulphur | Iron | Copper |

Calculations can be done using the simple equation:

$$\text{moles of atoms} = \frac{\text{mass}}{A_r}$$

The number of atoms in the mole, 6×10^{23} is called the **Avogadro constant**.

QUESTIONS

Q1 What is the kinetic theory of matter? Explain the structure of a liquid and a gas.

Q2 What is diffusion?

Q3 Comparing bromine molecules (mass = 160) and ammonia molecules (mass = 17), which will diffuse fastest and why?

More questions on the CD ROM

ATOMIC STRUCTURE

Sub-atomic particles

The smallest amount of an element that still behaves like that element is an **atom**. Each element has its own unique type of atom. Atoms are made up of smaller, sub-atomic particles. The three main sub-atomic particles are: **protons**, **neutrons** and **electrons**.

These particles are very small and have very little mass. However, it is possible to compare their masses using a **relative scale**. Their charges can also be compared in a similar way. The proton and neutron have the **same** mass, and the proton and electron have **opposite** charges.

Sub-atomic particle	Relative mass	Relative charge
proton	1	+1
neutron	1	0
electron	about $\frac{1}{2000}$	−1

Protons and neutrons are found in the centre of the atom, in a cluster called the **nucleus**. The electrons form a series of 'shells' around the nucleus.

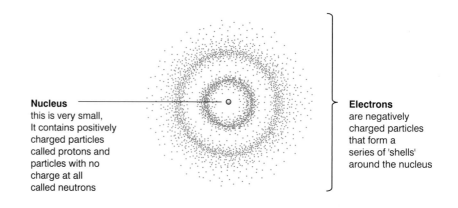

Nucleus
this is very small,
It contains positively
charged particles
called protons and
particles with no
charge at all
called neutrons

Electrons
are negatively
charged particles
that form a
series of 'shells'
around the nucleus

Atomic number and mass number

In order to describe the numbers of protons, neutrons and electrons in an atom, scientists use two numbers. These are called the **atomic number** and the **mass number**.

MASS NUMBER
(the number of
protons + neutrons)

symbol for
the element

$$_Z^A X$$

ATOMIC NUMBER
(the number of protons
which equals the number
of electrons)

The atomic number is used to order the elements in the periodic table. The atomic structures of the first ten elements are shown here.

Element	Atomic number	Mass number	Number of protons	Number of neutrons	Number of electrons
Hydrogen	1	1	1	0	1
Helium	2	4	2	2	2
Lithium	3	7	3	4	3
Beryllium	4	9	4	5	4
Boron	5	10	5	5	5
Carbon	6	12	6	6	6
Nitrogen	7	14	7	7	7
Oxygen	8	16	8	8	8
Fluorine	9	19	9	10	9
Neon	10	20	10	10	10

Hydrogen is the only atom that has **no neutrons**

Isotopes

Atoms of the same element with the **same number** of protons and electrons but **different** numbers of neutrons are called **isotopes**. For example, there are three isotopes of hydrogen:

Symbol	Number of neutrons
$^{1}_{1}H$	0
$^{2}_{1}H$	1
$^{3}_{1}H$	2

Isotopes have the same chemical properties but slightly different physical properties.

Relative atomic mass

The **relative atomic mass**, A_r is the average mass of a mole of atoms of an element on a scale where the mass of a carbon atom is 12 units. This takes into account the abundance of all the isotopes of that element that exist.

WORKED EXAMPLES

1 How many moles of atoms are there in 72 g of magnesium?
  (A_r of magnesium = 24)

Write down the formula:	moles $= \dfrac{\text{mass}}{A_r}$
Rearrange if necessary:	(None needed)
Substitute the numbers:	moles $= \dfrac{72}{24}$
Write the answer and units:	moles $= 3$ moles

2 What is the mass of 0.1 moles of carbon atoms? (A_r of carbon = 12)

Write down the formula:	$\text{moles} = \dfrac{\text{mass}}{A_r}$
Rearrange if necessary:	$\text{mass} = \text{moles} \times A_r$
Substitute the numbers:	$\text{mass} = 0.1 \times 12$
Write the answer and units:	$\text{mass} = 1.2 \text{ g}$

3 Chlorine has two isotopes, chlorine-35 of 75% abundance and chlorine-37 of 25% abundance. What is the relative atomic mass of chlorine?

The relative atomic mass of chlorine is:

$$\frac{(75 \times 35) + (25 \times 37)}{100} = 35.5.$$

The relative atomic mass of chlorine is 35.5 because of the relative abundances of its isotopes.

Arrangements of electrons in the atom

The electrons are arranged in **shells** around the nucleus. The shells do not all contain the same number of electrons – the shell nearest to the nucleus can only take two electrons, whereas the next one further from the nucleus can take eight.

Electron shell	Maximum number of electrons
1	2
2	8
3	18

Oxygen has an atomic number of 8, so has 8 electrons. Of these, 2 will be in the first shell and 6 will be in the second shell. This arrangement is written 2, 6. A phosphorus atom with an atomic number of 15 has 15 electrons, arranged 2, 8, 5.

The electron arrangements are very important as they determine the way that the atom reacts chemically.

Atom diagrams

The atomic structure of an atom can be shown simply in a diagram.

Atom diagrams for carbon and sulphur showing the number of protons and neutrons, and the electron arrangements.

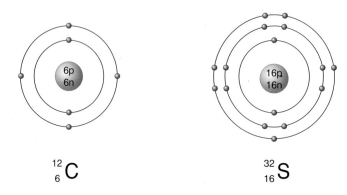

$$^{12}_{6}\text{C} \qquad\qquad ^{32}_{16}\text{S}$$

The arrangement of electrons in an atom is called its **electronic configuration**.

THE ELECTRONIC CONFIGURATION OF THE FIRST 20 ELEMENTS OF THE PERIODIC TABLE

There are 115 different elements. The elements can be arranged in a table, known as the Periodic Table, according to their chemical and physical properties. There is more about the Periodic Table on page 50.

The chemical properties of elements depend on the arrangement of electrons in the atoms. The electronic structure of the first twenty elements is shown in the table below.

Element	Symbol	Atomic number	Electron number	Electronic configuration
Hydrogen	H	1	1	1
Helium	He	2	2	2
Lithium	Li	3	3	2. 1
Beryllium	Be	4	4	2. 2
Boron	B	5	5	2. 3
Carbon	C	6	6	2. 4
Nitrogen	N	7	7	2. 5
Oxygen	O	8	8	2. 6
Fluorine	F	9	9	2. 7
Neon	Ne	10	10	2. 8
Sodium	Na	11	11	2. 8. 1
Magnesium	Mg	12	12	2. 8. 2
Aluminium	Al	13	13	2. 8. 3
Silicon	Si	14	14	2. 8. 4
Phosphorus	P	15	15	2. 8. 5
Sulphur	S	16	16	2. 8. 6
Chlorine	Cl	17	17	2. 8. 7
Argon	Ar	18	18	2. 8. 8
Potassium	K	19	19	2. 8. 8. 1
Calcium	Ca	20	20	2. 8. 8. 2

Periodicity and electronic configuration

In the Periodic Table (see page 50) lithium, sodium and potassium are placed on the left and neon and argon are placed on the right. As the atomic number increases from lithium to neon we are moving through a **period** of the Periodic table. The number of electrons in the outer shell increase. This is called **periodicity**.

Electronic configuration and chemical properties

Elements which have similar electronic configurations have similar chemical properties.

Lithium (2. 1), sodium (2. 8. 1) and potassium (2. 8. 8. 1) all have 1 electron in their outer shell. These are all highly reactive metals. They are called Group 1 elements in the Periodic Table

Fluorine (2. 7), chlorine (2. 8. 7), bromine (2. 8. 18. 7) and iodine (2. 8. 18. 7) all have 7 electrons in their outer shell. These elements are all highly reactive non-metals. They are called Group 7 elements, or halogens.

Neon lighting in Hong Kong.

The noble gases

The elements helium (2), neon (2. 8), argon (2. 8. 8), krypton (2. 8. 18. 8) and xenon (2. 8. 18. 18. 8) all have filled outer electron shells. These electronic configurations mean that these gases are extremely stable and unreactive, they are called Noble gases.

QUESTIONS

Q1 Calculate the number of moles in the following:
  a 56 g of silicon (Si = 28)
  b 3.1 g of phosphorus (P = 31)

Q2 Explain the meanings of:
  a atomic number
  b mass number.

Q3 Copy out and then complete the table.

Atom	Number of protons	Number of neutrons	Number of electrons	Electron arrangement
$^{28}_{14}$Si				
$^{24}_{12}$Mg				
$^{32}_{16}$S				
$^{40}_{18}$Ar				

Q4 The table below shows information about the structure of six particles (A–F).
  a In each of the questions i to v, choose one of the six particles A–F. Each letter may be used once, more than once or not at all.
  Choose a particle that:
    i   has a mass number of 12
    ii has the highest mass number
    iii has no overall charge
    iv has an overall positive charge
    v   is the same element as particle E.
  b Draw an atom diagram for particle F.

Particle	Protons (positive charge)	Neutrons (neutral)	Electrons (negative charge)
A	8	8	10
B	12	12	10
C	6	6	6
D	8	10	10
E	6	8	6
F	11	12	11

More questions on the CD ROM

RELATIVE FORMULA MASSES AND MOLAR VOLUMES

Relative formula masses, M_r, and relative atomic masses A_r

A relative formula mass can be worked out from the relative atomic masses of the atoms in the formula.

You can also refer to a mole of molecules. A mole of water molecules will be 6×10^{23} water molecules. The **relative formula mass** (M_r) of a molecule can be worked out by simply adding up the relative atomic masses of the atoms in the molecule. For example:

> Water, H_2O (H = 1, O = 16)
>
> The relative formula mass (M_r) = 1 + 1 + 16 = 18.
>
> Carbon dioxide, CO_2 (C = 12, O = 16)
>
> The RMM = 12 + 16 + 16 = 44.
>
> (Note: The '2' only applies to the oxygen atom.)

A similar approach can be used for any formula, including ionic formulae. As ionic compounds do not exist as molecules, the **relative formula mass** (M_r) can be worked out.

WORKED EXAMPLES

> Sodium chloride, NaCl (Na = 23, Cl = 35.5)
>
> The relative formula mass (M_r) = 23 + 35.5 = 58.5
>
> Potassium nitrate, KNO_3 (K = 39, N = 14, O = 16)
>
> M_r = 39 + 14 + 16 + 16 + 16 = 101
>
> (Note: The '3' only applies to the oxygen atoms.)
>
> Calcium hydroxide, $Ca(OH)_2$ (Ca = 40, O = 16, H = 1)
>
> M_r = 40 + (16 + 1)2 = 40 + 34 = 74
>
> (Note: The '2' applies to everything in the bracket.)
>
> Magnesium nitrate, $Mg(NO_3)_2$ (Mg = 24, N = 14, O = 16)
>
> M_r = 24 + (14 + 16 + 16 + 16)2 = 24 + (62)2 = 24 + 124 = 148

An equation can be written that can be used with atoms, molecules and ionic compounds.

> number of moles = $\dfrac{\text{mass}}{M_r}$

Amedeo Avogadro
(1776 – 1856)

Moles

A mole is an amount of substance. It is a very large number, approximately 6×10^{23}. This number is called the Avogadro constant.

For example, you can have a mole of atoms, a mole of molecules or a mole of electrons. A mole of atoms will be 6×10^{23} atoms.

The **relative atomic mass** of an element tells you the mass of a mole of atoms of that element. So for example a mole of carbon atoms has a mass of 12 grams.

The **relative formula mass** tells you the mass of a mole of that substance. So for example a mole of sodium chloride, NaCl, has a relative formula mass of 58.5 so the mole will have a mass of 58.5 g.

Moles of gases

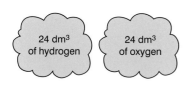

Each of these contains 1 mole (6×10^{23}) of molecules.

In reactions involving gases it is often more convenient to measure the **volume** of a gas rather than its mass.

There are many gases and they are of crucial importance. We often need to know the amount of a gas but it is difficult to weigh a gas. By using molar volumes we can find out the amount of a gas by using the volume of the gas rather than the mass.

The volume of one mole of any gas contains the Avogadro constant number of molecules (particles) of that gas. So this means that equal volumes of all gases taken at the same temperature and pressure must contain the same number of molecules. This is sometimes called **Avogadro's law**.

One mole of any gas occupies the same volume under the same conditions of temperature and pressure. The conditions chosen are usually room temperature (25 °C) and normal atmospheric pressure.

1 mole of any gas occupies 24 000 cm^3 (24 dm^3) at room temperature and pressure (rtp). 1 mole occupies 22.4 dm^3 at standard temperature and pressure (stp).

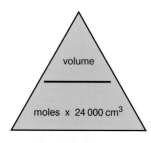

The triangle can be used as before to work out whether to multiply or divide the quantities.

The following equation can be used to convert moles and volumes:

$$\text{moles} = \frac{\text{volume in } cm^3}{24\,000}$$

WORKED EXAMPLES

What volume of hydrogen is formed at room temperature and pressure when 4 g of magnesium is added to excess dilute hydrochloric acid?
(H = 1, Mg = 24)

Equation: $Mg(s)$ + $2HCl(aq)$ → $MgCl_2(aq)$ + $H_2(g)$

Moles: 1   2   1   1

Masses/volumes: 24 g   24 000 cm^3

Number of moles magnesium = $\frac{4}{24}$ = 0.167

Therefore 0.167 moles hydrogen gas will be produced

Therefore volume of hydrogen gas = 0.167 × 24 000
                                 = 4000 cm^3

Note: The hydrochloric acid is in excess. This means that there is enough to react with all the magnesium.

What volume of carbon dioxide will be produced when 124 g of copper carbonate is broken down by heating?

Words: copper carbonate → copper oxide + carbon dioxide

Equation: $CuCO_3(s) \rightarrow CuO(s) + CO_2(g)$

Moles: 1   1   1

Masses/vols: 124 g

The relative formula mass of $CuCO_3$ is 64 + 12 + (3 × 16) = 124 g

So there is exactly one mole of reactant, so there must be one mole of products produced. In other words, one mole of CO_2 is produced, so since one mole of any gas has a volume of 24 dm^3, this amount of carbon dioxide is produced.

Values of molar volumes at different temperatures and pressures

Room temperature and pressure: rtp means 25°C and normal atmospheric pressure.

Standard temperature and pressure: stp means 0°C and normal atmospheric pressure.

The molar volume of a gas at rtp is 24 dm^3.

The molar volume of a gas at stp is 22.4 dm^3.

A* EXTRA

- You might be asked to use the molar volume of a gas at stp or rtp. Make sure you read the Question carefully.

QUESTIONS

Q1 How many moles are in the following?
a 64 g of S_8
b 9.8 g of H_2SO_4
c 21 g of Li

($S = 32$; $H = 1$; $O = 16$; $Li = 7$)

Q2 What is the mass of the following?
a 2.5 moles of Sr
b 0.25 moles of MgO
c 0.1 moles of C_2H_5Br

($Sr = 88$; $Mg = 24$; $O = 16$; $C = 12$; $H = 1$; $Br = 80$)

Q3 Iron(III) oxide is reduced to iron by carbon monoxide.

($C = 12$, $O = 16$, $Fe = 56$)

$$Fe_2O_3(s) + 3CO(g) \rightarrow 2Fe(s) + 3CO_2(g)$$

a Calculate the mass of iron that could be obtained by the reduction of 800 tonnes of iron(III) oxide.
b What volume of carbon dioxide would be obtained by the reduction of 320 g of iron(III) oxide?

More questions
on the CD ROM

CHEMICAL FORMULAE AND CHEMICAL EQUATIONS

Experiments to find the formulae of simple compounds

Videos & questions on the CD ROM

FINDING THE FORMULA OF MAGNESIUM OXIDE

Magnesium ribbon can be heated in a crucible to make a white powder which is called magnesium oxide. The magnesium reacts with oxygen from the air. The reaction is called **oxidation** because a substance combines with oxygen.

If you measure the masses of the reactants in this reaction, you can use the relative atomic masses to work out the formula of the compound made.

Here are some typical results when 2.4 g of magnesium is oxidised.

Measurement	Value
Crucible + lid	30.0 g
Crucible + lid + magnesium	32.4 g
crucible + lid + magnesium oxide	34.0 g
magnesium	32.4 – 30.0 = 2.4 g
magnesium oxide	34.0 – 30.0 = 4.0 g
oxygen	4.0 – 2.4 g = 1.6 g

The result is that 2.4 g of magnesium joins with 1.6 g of oxygen. Therefore 24 g of magnesium would join with 16 g of oxygen. The relative atomic mass of magnesium is 24, and of oxygen is 16. So 1 mole of magnesium atoms joins with 1 mole of oxygen atoms. This means that the formula of magnesium oxide is simply MgO.

Magnesium ribbon is put in a crucible with a lid on it. The crucible is heated until the magnesium is red hot. The lid is lifted and put back down again to allow oxygen in. This lets the magnesium burn but prevents loss of magnesium oxide.

WORKED EXAMPLE

Copper (II) oxide can be heated in hydrogen to produce copper and water.
In an experiment 12.8 g of copper was produced from 16.0 g of copper oxide.

Relative atomic masses: (H = 1, O = 16, Cu = 64).

Word equation: copper oxide + hydrogen → copper + water

Masses   16.0 g   12.8 g

So the mass of oxygen that was combined with the copper = 16.0 – 12.8 = 3.2 g

Therefore 32 g of oxygen would be combined with 128 g of copper.

Therefore = $\frac{32}{16}$ = 2 moles of oxygen would be combined with $\frac{128}{64}$ = 2 moles of copper.

Therefore 1 mole of oxygen would be combined with 1 mole of copper.

Therefore the formula for copper oxide is CuO.

Finding the formula of water

Your teacher may have shown you an experiment where an electric current is passed through water (it is actually a dilute solution of sulphuric acid). When the power is turned on, gases are collected from the water at the two electrodes. After half an hour about twice as much gas is collected at the negative terminal (cathode) as at the positive terminal (anode).

The gas collected at the cathode is hydrogen and the gas collected at the anode is oxygen.

Remember that one mole of any gas occupies the same volume at the same pressure.

So because twice as much hydrogen is produced as oxygen, this shows that the formula for water must be H_2O.

The formulae of many compounds can be obtained experimentally.

Using moles of atoms to find chemical formulae

A chemical formula shows the number of atoms of each element that combine together. For example:

H_2O A water molecule contains 2 hydrogen atoms and 1 oxygen atom.

Alternatively:

H_2O 1 mole of water molecules is made from 2 moles of hydrogen atoms and 1 mole of oxygen atoms.

The formula of a compound can be calculated if the number of moles of the combining elements are known.

WORKED EXAMPLES

1 What is the simplest formula of a hydrocarbon that contains 60 g of carbon combined with 20 g of hydrogen? (A_rs: H = 1, C = 12)

	C	H
Write down the mass of each element:	60	20
Work out the number of moles of each element:	$\frac{60}{12} = 5$	$\frac{20}{1} = 20$
Find the simplest ratio (divide by the smaller number):	$\frac{5}{5} = 1$	$\frac{20}{5} = 4$
Write the formula showing the ratio of atoms:	CH_4	

2 What is the simplest formula of calcium carbonate if it contains 40% calcium, 12% carbon and 48% oxygen? (C = 12, O = 16, Ca = 40)

	Ca	C	O
Write down the mass of each element:	40	12	48
Work out the number of moles of each element:	$\frac{40}{40} = 1$	$\frac{12}{12} = 1$	$\frac{48}{16} = 3$
Find the simplest ratio:	(Already in the simplest ratio)		
Write the formula showing the ratio of atoms:	$CaCO_3$		

A* EXTRA

- When calculating moles of elements, you must be careful to make sure you know what the question is referring to. For example, you may be asked for the mass of 1 mole of nitrogen gas. N = 14, but nitrogen gas is diatomic, i.e. N_2, so the mass of 1 mole N_2 = 28 g. This also applies to other diatomic elements, e.g. Cl_2, Br_2, I_2, O_2 and H_2.

Formulae such as CH_4 and $CaCO_3$ are called **empirical formulae**. This means that the formula shows the simplest ratio of the atoms present.

Now consider the substance **ethane**. The formula for ethane is C_2H_6. The simplest ratio of the atoms in ethane would be CH_3. But this substance cannot exist. The formula C_2H_6 shows the actual number of atoms of each element in one molecule of ethane.

This is called the **molecular formula**.

Percentage yield and percentage purity

When you prepare chemicals using chemical reactions the substances that are formed are called the **products**. The amount of product you get is called the **yield**.

Sometimes the yield is less than you would expect. There may be some product left behind at different stages in the preparation.

A useful way of comparing the yields from different processes is to find the **percentage yield**. To do this, the chemist measures the actual yield (how much you actually made), works out the predicted yield for the reaction and uses this formula:

$$\text{percentage yield} = \frac{\text{actual yield}}{\text{predicted yield}} \times 100$$

WORKED EXAMPLE

If 25 cm^3 of ammonium hydroxide solution reacts to form the fertiliser ammonium sulphate, the predicted yield is 3.30 g.

However, when chemists actually made this they only found 2.64 g as the actual mass produced.

$$\begin{aligned}
\text{percentage yield} &= \frac{\text{actual yield}}{\text{predicted yield}} \times 100 \\
&= \frac{2.64}{3.30} \times 100 \\
&= 80\%.
\end{aligned}$$

The percentage purity measures how pure a substance is.

$$\text{percentage purity} = \frac{\text{amount of pure substance}}{\text{total amount of substance}} \times 100$$

Writing chemical equations

In a **chemical equation** the starting chemicals are called the **reactants** and the finishing chemicals are called the **products**.

Follow these simple rules to write a chemical equation.

1 Write down the **word equation**.

2 Write down the **symbols** (for elements) and **formulae** (for compounds).

3 **Balance the equation**, to make sure there are the same number of each type of atom on each side of the equation.

Many elements are **diatomic**. They exist as molecules containing two atoms.

Element	Form in which it exists
hydrogen	H_2
oxygen	O_2
nitrogen	N_2
chlorine	Cl_2
bromine	Br_2
iodine	I_2

WORKED EXAMPLES

1 When a lighted splint is put into a test tube of hydrogen the hydrogen burns with a 'pop'. In fact the hydrogen reacts with oxygen in the air (the reactants) to form water (the product). Write the chemical equation for this reaction.

Word equation:	hydrogen + oxygen → water
Symbols and formulae:	$H_2 + O_2 \rightarrow H_2O$
Balance the equation:	$2H_2 + O_2 \rightarrow 2H_2O$

For every two molecules of hydrogen that react, one molecule of oxygen is needed and two molecules of water are formed.

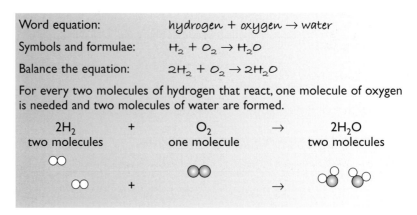

$2H_2$	+	O_2	→	$2H_2O$
two molecules		one molecule		two molecules

2 What is the equation when sulphur burns in air?

Word equation:	sulphur + oxygen → sulphur dioxide
Symbols and formulae:	$S + O_2 \rightarrow SO_2$
Balance the equation:	$S + O_2 \rightarrow SO_2$

Methane is burning in the oxygen in the air to form carbon dioxide and water.

Balancing equations

Balancing equations can be quite tricky. Basically it is done by trial and error. However, the golden rule is that **balancing numbers can only be put in front of the formulae.**

For example, to balance the equation for the reaction between methane and oxygen:

	Reactants	Products
Start with the unbalanced equation.	$CH_4 + O_2$	$CO_2 + H_2O$
Count the number of atoms on each side of the equation.	$1C$ ✓, $4H$, $2O$	$1C$ ✓, $2H$, $3O$
There is a need to increase the number of H atoms on the products side of the equation. Put a '2' in front of the H_2O.	$CH_4 + O_2$	$CO_2 + 2H_2O$
Count the number of atoms on each side of the equation again.	$1C$ ✓, $4H$ ✓, $2O$	$1C$ ✓, $4H$ ✓, $4O$
There is a need to increase the number of O atoms on the reactant side of the equation. Put a '2' in front of the O_2.	$CH_4 + 2O_2$	$CO_2 + 2H_2O$
Count the atoms on each side of the equation again.	$1C$ ✓, $4H$ ✓, $4O$ ✓	$1C$ ✓, $4H$ ✓, $4O$ ✓

No atoms have been created or destroyed in the reaction. The equation is balanced!

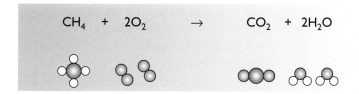

$$CH_4 + 2O_2 \rightarrow CO_2 + 2H_2O$$

The number of each type of atom is the same on the left and right sides of the equation.

In balancing equations involving **radicals** you can use the same procedure. For example, when lead(II) nitrate solution is mixed with potassium iodide solution, lead(II) iodide and potassium nitrate are produced.

1 Words:
lead(II) nitrate + potassium iodide → lead(II) iodide + potassium nitrate

2 Symbols:
$Pb(NO_3)_2$ + KI → PbI_2 + KNO_3

3 Balance the nitrates:
$Pb(NO_3)_2$ + KI → PbI_2 + $2KNO_3$

Balance the iodides:
$Pb(NO_3)_2$ + $2KI$ → PbI_2 + $2KNO_3$

This reaction occurs simply on mixing the solutions of lead(II) nitrate and potassium iodide. Lead iodide is an insoluble yellow compound.

State	State symbol
solid	s
liquid	l
gas	g
solution	aq

States and their symbols.

A* EXTRA

- You must be able to write balanced chemical equations. Practise working out the balanced equation whenever you come across a reaction in this course.

Ionic equations

Here is a table showing the charges on some ions

Positive ions (cations)		Negative ions (anions)	
ammonium	NH_4^+	bromide	Br^-
hydrogen	H^+	chloride	Cl^-
copper(I)	Cu^+	iodide	I^-
potassium	K^+	hydroxide	OH^-
sodium	Na^+	nitrate	NO_3^-
silver	Ag^+	carbonate	CO_3^{2-}
calcium	Ca^{2+}	oxide	O^{2-}
magnesium	Mg^{2+}	sulphate	SO_4^{2-}
copper(II)	Cu^{2+}	sulphite	SO_3^{2-}
iron(II)	Fe^{2+}	sulphide	S^{2-}
zinc	Zn^{2+}	phosphate	PO_4^{3-}
aluminium	Al^{3+}		
iron(III)	Fe^{3+}		

Ionic equations show reactions involving **ions** (atoms or radicals that have lost or gained electrons). The size of the charge on an ion is the same as the combining power – whether it is positive or negative depends on which part of the periodic table the element is placed in.

In many ionic reactions some of the ions play no part in the reaction. These ions are called **spectator ions**. A simplified ionic equation can therefore be written, using only the important, reacting ions. In equations, **state symbols** are used and appear in brackets.

The equation must **balance** in terms of chemical symbols and charges.

WORKED EXAMPLES

1 In the reaction given to produce lead(II) iodide, the potassium and nitrate ions are spectators – the important ions are the lead(II) ions and the iodide ions.

The simplified ionic equation is:

$$Pb^{2+}(aq) + 2I^-\,(aq) \rightarrow PbI_2(s)$$

Balance the equation:

	Reactants	Products
	$Pb^{2+}(aq) + 2I^-$ (aq)	$PbI_2(s)$
symbols	1Pb ✓, 2I ✓	1Pb ✓, 2I ✓
charges	2^+ and $2^- = 0$ ✓	0 ✓

The equation shows that any solution containing lead(II) ions will react with any solution containing iodide ions to form lead(II) iodide.

2 Any solution containing copper(II) ions and any solution containing hydroxide ions can be used to make copper(II) hydroxide, which appears as a solid:

$$Cu^{2+}(aq) + 2OH^-(aq) \rightarrow Cu(OH)_2(s)$$

	Reactants	**Products**
	$Cu^{2+}(aq) + 2OH^-(aq)$	$Cu(OH)_2(s)$
symbols	1 Cu ✓, 2 O ✓, 2 H ✓	1 Cu ✓, 2 O ✓, 2 H ✓
charges	2^+ and $2^- = 0$ ✓	0 ✓

Linking reactants and products

Chemical equations allow quantities of **reactants** and **products** to be linked together. They tell you how much of the products you can expect to make from a fixed amount of reactants.

In a balanced equation the numbers in front of each symbol or formula indicate the number of moles represented. The number of moles can then be converted into a mass in grams.

For example, when magnesium (A_r 24) reacts with oxygen (A_r 16):

Write down the balanced equation:	$2Mg(s)$	+	$O_2(g)$	$\rightarrow$	$2MgO(s)$
Write down the number of moles:	2	+	1	$\rightarrow$	2
Convert moles to masses:	48 g	+	32 g	$\rightarrow$	80 g

So when 48 g of magnesium reacts with 32 g of oxygen, 80 g of magnesium oxide is produced. From this you should be able to work out the mass of magnesium oxide produced from any mass of magnesium.

WORKED EXAMPLES

1 What mass of magnesium oxide can be made from 6 g of magnesium? (O = 16, Mg = 24)

Equation:	$2Mg(s)$	+	$O_2(g)$	$\rightarrow$	$2MgO(s)$
Moles:	2		1		2
Masses:	48 g		32 g		80 g

6 g magnesium $\rightarrow \dfrac{6}{24} = 0.25$ moles magnesium

Therefore 0.25 moles magnesium oxide formed

Therefore $0.25 \times 40 = 10$ g

Note: In this example, there was no need to work out the mass of oxygen needed. It was assumed that there would be as much as was necessary to convert all the magnesium to magnesium oxide.

In an oxidation reaction, magnesium gives fireworks and flares a brilliant white colour.

2 What mass of ammonia can be made from 56 g of nitrogen?
(H = 1, N = 14)

Equation:			$N_2(g)$	+	$3H_2(g)$	$\rightarrow$	$2NH_3(g)$
Moles:			1		3		2
Masses:			28 g		6 g		34 g
Moles nitrogen	$= \frac{56}{28} = 2$						
Moles ammonia	$= 2 \times 2 = 4$						
Mass ammonia	$= 4 \times 17 = 68g$						

Note: In this example there was no need to work out the mass of hydrogen required.

Moles of solutions

A solution is made when a **solute** dissolves in a **solvent**. The concentration of a solution depends on how much solute is dissolved in how much solvent. The concentrations of a solution is defined in terms of moles per litre (1000 cm^3), or mol dm^{-3}.

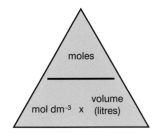

This triangle will help you to calculate concentrations of solutions.

1 mole of solute dissolved to make 1000 cm^3 of solution produces a 1 mol dm^{-3} solution

2 moles dissolved to make a 1000 cm^3 solution produces a 2 mol dm^{-3} solution

0.5 moles dissolved to make a 1000 cm^3 solution produces a 0.5 mol dm^{-3} solution

1 mole dissolved to make a 500 cm^3 solution produces a 2 mol dm^{-3} solution

1 mole dissolved to make a 250 cm^3 solution produces a 4 mol dm^{-3} solution.

If the same amount of solute is dissolved to make a smaller volume of solution, the solution will be more concentrated.

WORKED EXAMPLE
How much sodium chloride can be made from reacting 100 cm^3 of 1.0 mol dm^{-3} hydrochloric acid with excess sodium hydroxide solution?
(Na = 23, Cl = 35.5)

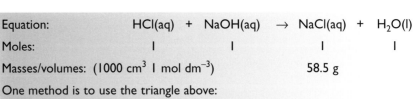

One method is to use the triangle above:

i.e. moles = 1 mol dm^{-3} × 0.1 dm^3
= 0.1

1 mole NaCl = 58.5 g

0.1 mole NaCl = 5.85 g

Note: 100 cm^3 of 1 mol dm^{-3} solution is equal to 0.1 mole.

QUESTIONS

Q1 Write symbol equations from the following word equations:
a carbon + oxygen → carbon dioxide
b iron + oxygen → iron(III) oxide
c iron(III) oxide + carbon → iron + carbon dioxide
d calcium carbonate + hydrochloric acid → calcium chloride + carbon dioxide + water.

Q2 Write ionic equations for the following reactions:
a calcium ions and carbonate ions form calcium carbonate
b iron(II) ions and hydroxide ions form iron(II) hydroxide
c silver(I) ions and bromide ions form silver(I) bromide.

Q3 What mass of sodium hydroxide can be made by reacting 2.3 g of sodium with water? (H = 1, O = 16, Na = 23)

$$2Na(s) + 2H_2O(l) \rightarrow 2NaOH(aq) + H_2(g)$$

Q4 What mass of barium sulphate can be produced from 50 cm^3 of 0.2 mol dm^{-3} barium chloride solution and excess sodium sulphate solution?
(O = 16, S = 32, Ba = 137)

$$BaCl_2(aq) + Na_2SO_4(aq) \rightarrow BaSO_4(s) + 2NaCl(aq)$$

Q5 Titanium chloride contains 25% titanium and 75% chlorine by mass. Work out the simplest formula of titanium chloride.
(Ti = 48, Cl = 35.5)

Q6 Calculate the formulae of the following compounds:
a 2.3 g of sodium reacting with 8.0 g of bromine
(Na = 23, Br = 80).
b 0.6 g of carbon reacting with oxygen to make 2.2 g of compound
c 11.12 g of iron reacting with chlorine to make 32.20 g of compound

More questions on the CD ROM

IONIC COMPOUNDS

The formation of ions

Atoms bond together with other atoms in a chemical reaction to make a compound. For example, sodium will react with chlorine to make sodium chloride. Hydrogen will react with oxygen to make water.

Ions are formed from atoms by the gain or loss of electrons. Both metal and non-metals try to achieve complete outer electron shells.

Metals lose electrons from their outer shells and form **positive ions**.

Non-metals gain electrons into their outer shells and form **negative ions**.

The ions are held together by strong electrostatic forces.

The bonding process can be represented in **dot-and-cross diagrams**. Look at the reaction between sodium and chlorine as an example.

Sodium is a metal. It has an atomic number of 11 and so has 11 electrons, arranged 2, 8, 1. Its atom diagram looks like this:

Chlorine is a non-metal. It has an atomic number of 17 and so has 17 electrons, arranged 2, 8, 7. Its atom diagram looks like this:

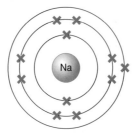 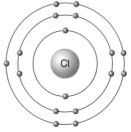

Sodium has one electron in its outer shell. It can achieve a full outer shell by losing this electron. The sodium atom transfers its outermost electron to the chlorine atom.

Chlorine has seven electrons in its outer shell. It can achieve a full outer shell by gaining an extra electron. The chlorine atom accepts an electron from the sodium.

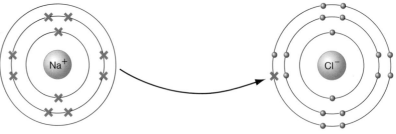

The sodium is no longer an atom; it is now an ion. It does not have equal numbers of protons and electrons, it is no longer neutral. It has one more proton than it has electrons, so it is a positive ion with a charge of 1+. The ion is written as Na^+.

The chlorine is no longer an atom; it is now an ion. It does not have equal numbers of protons and electrons, it is no longer neutral. It has one more electron than protons, so it is a negative ion with a charge of 1–. The ion is written as Cl^-.

METALS CAN TRANSFER MORE THAN ONE ELECTRON TO A NON-METAL

Magnesium combines with oxygen to form **magnesium oxide**. The magnesium (electron arrangement 2, 8, 2) transfers two electrons to the oxygen (electron arrangement 2, 6). Magnesium therefore forms a Mg^{2+} ion and oxygen forms an O^{2-} ion.

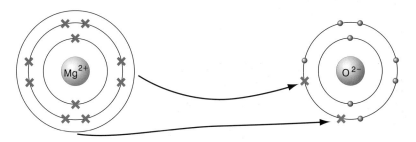

Aluminium has an electron arrangement 2, 8, 3. When it combines with fluorine with an electron arrangement 2, 7, three fluorine atoms are needed for each aluminium atom. The formula of **aluminium fluoride** is therefore AlF_3.

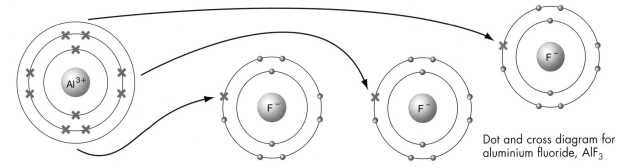

Dot and cross diagram for aluminium fluoride, AlF_3

<table>
<tr><td>

A* EXTRA

- In ionic bonding the oxygen atom gains two electrons and changes into the oxide ion (O^{2-}). In this way, the oxygen atom is reduced by the addition of the electrons.

</td></tr>
</table>

Dot and cross diagram for magnesium oxide, MgO

Electronic configuration and ionic charge

When atoms form ions they want to achieve stable electronic configurations. Here are some common ions and their electronic configurations:

Ion	Electronic configuration
Li^+	2
Na^+	2. 8
Mg^{2+}	2. 8
F^-	2. 8
Cl^-	2. 8. 8
O^{2-}	2. 8

Properties of ionic compounds

Ionic compounds have high melting points and high boiling points because of strong electrostatic forces between ions.

The strong electrostatic attraction between oppositely charged ions is called an ionic bond.

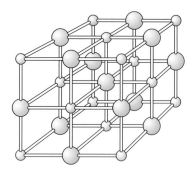

chloride ion   sodium ion

In solid sodium chloride, the ions are held firmly in place – they are not free to move. Ionic compounds have giant ionic lattice structures like this.

Crystals of sodium chloride.

Ionic compounds form **giant lattice structures.** For example, when sodium chloride is formed by ionic bonding, the ions do not pair up. Each sodium ion is surrounded by six chloride ions, and each chloride ion is surrounded by six sodium ions.

The electrostatic attractions between the ions are very strong. The properties of sodium chloride can be explained using this model of its structure.

Properties of sodium chloride	Explanation in terms of structure
Hard crystals	Strong forces between the ions
High melting point (801°C)	Strong forces between the ions
Dissolves in water	The water is also able to form strong electrostatic attractions with the ions – the ions are 'plucked' off the lattice structure
Does not conduct electricity when solid	Strong forces between the ions prevent them from moving
Does conduct electricity when molten or dissolved in water	The strong forces between the ions have been broken down and so the ions are able to move

A* EXTRA

- Ionic compounds are electrolytes. They conduct electricity when molten or when dissolved in water (i.e. when the ions are free to move).
- Insoluble compounds such as barium sulphate will only conduct electricity when they are molten.

Magnesium oxide is another ionic compound. Its ionic formula is $Mg^{2+}O^{2-}$.

MgO has a much higher melting point and boiling point than NaCl because of the increased charges on the ions. The forces holding the ions together are greater in MgO than in NaCl.

QUESTIONS

Q1 For each of the following reactions say whether the compound formed is ionic or not:
- a hydrogen and chlorine
- b carbon and hydrogen
- c sodium and oxygen
- d chlorine and oxygen
- e calcium and bromine.

Q2 Write down the ions formed by the following elements:
- a potassium
- b aluminium
- c sulphur
- d fluorine.

Q3 Explain why an ionic substance such as potassium chloride:
- a has a high melting point
- b behaves as an electrolyte.

More questions
on the CD ROM

COVALENT SUBSTANCES

How covalent bonds are formed

Covalent bonding involves electron sharing. It occurs between atoms of non-metals. It results in the formation of a **molecule**. The non-metal atoms try to achieve complete outer electron shells.

A **single covalent bond** is formed when two atoms each contribute one electron to a **shared pair** of electrons. For example, hydrogen gas exists as H_2 molecules. Each hydrogen atom needs to fill its electron shell. They can do this by sharing electrons.

The dot-and-cross diagram and displayed formula of H_2.

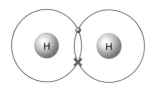

represented as

H—H

A covalent bond is the result of attraction between the bond pair of electrons (negative charges) and the nuclei (positive charges) of the atoms involved in the bond. A single covalent bond can be represented by a single line. The formula of the molecule can be written as a **displayed formula**, H—H. The hydrogen and oxygen atoms in water are also held together by single covalent bonds.

Water contains single covalent bonds.

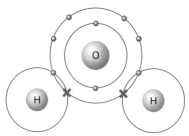

The hydrogen and carbon atoms in methane are held together by single covalent bonds.

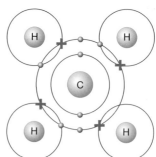

The hydrogen chloride, HCl molecule is also held together by a single covalent bond.

Ethane has a slightly more complex electron arrangement.

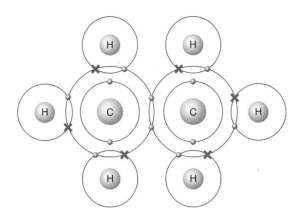

Some molecules contain **double covalent bonds**. In carbon dioxide, the carbon atom has an electron arrangement of 2, 4 and needs an additional four electrons to complete its outer electron shell. It needs to share its four electrons with four electrons from oxygen atoms (electron arrangement 2, 6). Two oxygen atoms are needed, each sharing two electrons with the carbon atom.

Some molecules contain **triple covalent bonds**. In the nitrogen molecule, each nitrogen atom has an electron arrangement of 2. 5 and needs an additional three electrons to complete its outer electron shell. It needs to share three of its outer electrons with another nitrogen atom. This forms a triple bond.

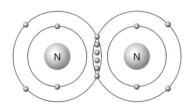

The shapes of molecules

Carbon dioxide is a linear molecule $\quad o = c = o$

A **water** molecule is V-shaped.

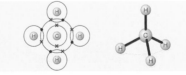

The **methane** molecule is tetrahedral in shape.

in **ammonia** one nitrogen atom is bonded to three hydrogen atoms. The ammonia molecule is a pyramidal shape.

Molecular crystals

Covalent compounds can form simple molecular crystals. Many covalent crystals only exist in the solid form at low temperatures. Some simple molecular crystals are ice, solid carbon dioxide, solid methane, solid ammonia and iodine.

Properties of covalent compounds

Substances with molecular structures ae usually gases, liquids or solids with low melting points and boiling points.

Covalent bonds are also strong bonds. They are **intramolecular** bonds – formed *within* each molecule. Much weaker intermolecular forces attract the individual molecules to each other.

The properties of covalent compounds can be explained using a simple model involving these two types of bond or forces.

Properties of hydrogen	Explanation in terms of structure	
Hydrogen is a gas with a very low melting point (−259 °C)	The intermolecular forces between the molecules are weak	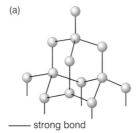
Hydrogen does not conduct electricity	There are no ions or free electrons present. The covalent bond (intramolecular bond) is a strong bond and the electrons cannot be easily removed from it	

Diamond and graphite

Some covalently bonded compounds do not exist as simple molecular structures in the way that hydrogen does. Diamond, for example, exists as a **giant structure** with each carbon atom covalently bonded to four others. The bonding is extremely strong – diamond has a melting point of about 3730 °C. Another form of carbon is graphite. Graphite has a different giant structure as seen in the diagram. Different forms of the same element are called **allotropes**.

(a) In diamond, each carbon atom forms four strong covalent bonds.

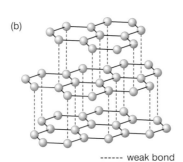

(b) In graphite, each carbon atom forms three strong covalent bonds and one weak intermolecular bond.

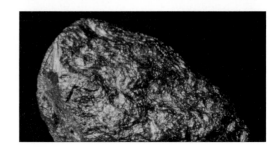

In graphite, carbon atoms form layers of hexagons in the plane of their strong covalent bonds. The weak bonds are between the layers. Because the layers can slide over each other, graphite is flaky and can be used as a lubricant. Graphite can conduct electricity because the electrons in the plane of the layers of hexagons are free to move along the layers.

In diamond, all the bonding is extremely strong and this makes diamond an extremely hard substance, one of the hardest substances known. This is why diamonds are used in cutting.

The atoms in both diamond and graphite are held together by strong covalent bonds which result in very high sublimation points.

Diamond and graphite mining

How are diamonds mined if diamond is the hardest structure?

Diamond is the hardest naturally occurring material in the world. Its hardness and high melting point make it ideal for industrial drill bits e.g. drilling for oil and gas.

Diamonds and graphite are mined throughout Africa. The diamond ore is called **kimberlite** and diamonds are found in kimberlite gravels and pipe formations. The Venetia mine in South Africa is in Messina in the Northern Province. It is the country's largest diamond producer.

After mining the ore is crushed, washed and screened using X-ray techniques to find the diamonds. Finally the diamonds are hand sorted and then washed and classified for sale.

Diamond mining and recovery is a clean operation. Processing of the ore uses no toxic chemicals and produces no chemical pollutants.

Drilling at night in the open pit at the Venetia mine in South Africa.

QUESTIONS

Q1 Draw dot-and-cross diagrams to show the bonding in the following compounds:
  a methane, CH_4
  b oxygen, O_2
  c nitrogen, N_2
  d potassium sulphide
  e lithium oxide.

Q2 Use the structure of graphite to explain
  a how carbon fibres can add strength to tennis racquets
  b how graphite conducts electricity.

Q3 Explain why methane (CH_4), which has strong covalent bonds between the carbon atom and the hydrogen atoms, has a very low melting point.

More questions on the CD ROM

ELECTROLYSIS

Electrolytes and non-electrolytes

Substances that can conduct electricity are called **electrolytes**. Experiments can be carried out using a simple electrical cell, and the size of the voltage produced shows how strong the electrolyte is.

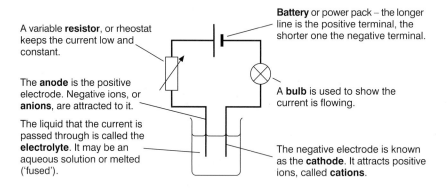

A variable **resistor**, or rheostat keeps the current low and constant.

Battery or power pack – the longer line is the positive terminal, the shorter one the negative terminal.

The **anode** is the positive electrode. Negative ions, or **anions**, are attracted to it.

A **bulb** is used to show the current is flowing.

The liquid that the current is passed through is called the **electrolyte**. It may be an aqueous solution or melted ('fused').

The negative electrode is known as the **cathode**. It attracts positive ions, called **cations**.

Conditions for electrolysis

The substance being electrolysed (the **electrolyte**) must contain ions and these ions must be free to move. In other words, the substance must either be molten or dissolved in water.

A d.c. voltage must be used. The **electrode** connected to the **positive** terminal of the power supply is known as the **anode**. The electrode connected to the **negative** terminal of the power supply is known as the **cathode**. The electrical circuit can be drawn as shown below.

A typical electrical circuit used in electrolysis.

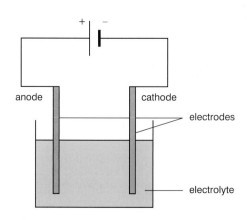

anode   cathode

electrodes

electrolyte

How does the electrolyte change?

The negative ions are attracted to the anode and release electrons.
(Loss of electrons is oxidation.) For example:

chloride ions → chlorine molecules + electrons
$$2Cl^-(aq) \rightarrow Cl_2(g) + 2e^-$$

The positive ions are attracted to the cathode and gain electrons.
(Gaining electrons is reduction.) For example:

copper ions + electrons → copper atoms
$$Cu^{2+}(aq) + 2e^- \rightarrow Cu(s)$$

The electrons move through the external circuit from the anode to
the cathode.

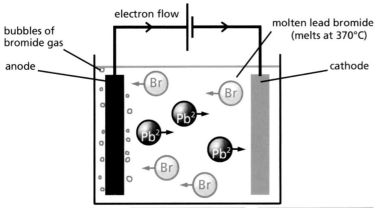

Electrolysis of molten
lead bromide

Negative bromide ions are drawn to the anode by electrostatic attraction. Each of two bromide ions loses an electron to the anode. $2Br^-(l) \rightarrow Br_2(l) + 2e^-$ The bromide ions are **discharged** and two bromide atoms join together to become a molecule of bromine.	The fumes of bromine and the compounds of lead formed are toxic, so this experiment must be performed in a fume cupboard.	Positive lead ions are drawn to the cathode by electrostatic attraction. Each ion gains two electrons from the cathode: $Pb^{2+}(l) + 2e^- \rightarrow Pb(l)$ The lead ion loses its charge - it is **discharged** and becomes a lead atom.

The equations shown in the figure above are known as **ionic half
equations**. Note that the number of electrons gained from the cathode is
the same as the number of electrons lost to the anode. This maintains an
electrical balance in the process. Electrons lost at the anode are
continually 'pumped' by the battery or power pack round to the cathode.

Another example of the electrolysis of a fused or melted compound is that
of sodium chloride. When solid sodium chloride is melted and electrolysed,
it is broken down to sodium and chlorine. This process is the only
practicable way of manufacturing sodium metal. Because both sodium and
chlorine are very reactive elements, it is important that once they are
discharged at the electrodes, they are kept apart to prevent them reacting
together again.

The Faraday

A **Faraday** is one mole of electrons. We use the Faraday when we carry out chemical calculations about electrolysis.

Ionic half equations

In electrolysis, the reactions at the electrodes can be shown as ionic **half equations**.

For example, when copper is deposited at the **cathode** the ionic half equation can be written as:

$$Cu^{2+}(aq) + 2e^- \rightarrow Cu(s)$$

The symbol e^- stands for an **electron**. At the cathode, positive ions gain electrons and become neutral. The equation must **balance** in terms of symbols and charges.

A typical reaction at the **anode** during electrolysis would be:

$$2Cl^-(aq) \rightarrow Cl_2(g) + 2e^-$$

In this reaction two chloride ions combine to form one molecule of chlorine, releasing two electrons.

WORKED EXAMPLE

Copper is purified using electrolysis.

The impure copper is made the anode in a cell with copper(II) sulphate as an electrolyte. The cathode is made from a thin piece of pure copper.

At the anode the copper atoms dissolve, forming copper ions:

copper atoms	$\rightarrow$	copper ions	+	electrons
Cu(s)	$\rightarrow$	$Cu^{2+}(aq)$	+	$2e^-$

At the cathode the copper ions are deposited to form copper atoms:

copper ions	+	electrons	$\rightarrow$	copper atoms
$Cu^{2+}(aq)$	+	$2e^-$	$\rightarrow$	Cu(s)

Copper is purified by electrolysis.

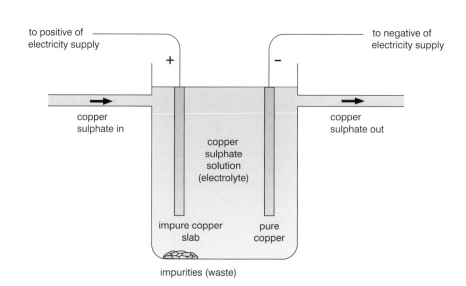

to positive of electricity supply

to negative of electricity supply

copper sulphate in

copper sulphate out

copper sulphate solution (electrolyte)

impure copper slab

pure copper

impurities (waste)

The half equation shows that 1 mole of Cu(II) ions reacts with 2 Faradays of electrons. 1 mole of copper will be produced. This will be 63.5 g of copper. More detail about the purification of copper is shown on page 44.

Electrolysis in industry

The principles of electrolysis are used in industry to make a wide variety of chemicals that in turn are used to make many everyday materials.

WHAT HAPPENS WHEN BRINE IS ELECTROLYSED?

One of the earliest applications of electrolysis was that of sodium chloride solution. In places where underground salt deposits were discovered, this was dissolved, pumped to the surface and electrolysed. Because of the many useful chemicals that can be produced in this process, several sites where such salt deposits occur have evolved into large complexes for the chemical industry.

Electrolysis of brine is usually carried out in a **diaphragm cell**, where the electrodes are arranged in layers. The diaphragm that separates the layers also helps prevent the hydrogen and chlorine gases from mixing and reacting together.

Electrolysis of brine in a diaphragm cell.

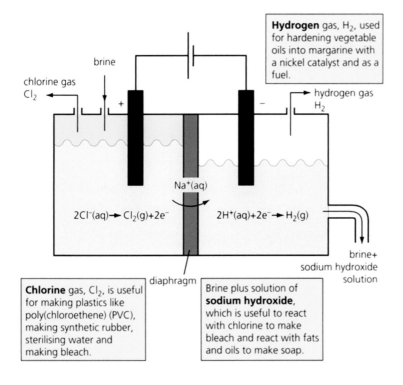

Hydrogen gas, H_2, used for hardening vegetable oils into margarine with a nickel catalyst and as a fuel.

chlorine gas Cl_2

brine

hydrogen gas H_2

$Na^+(aq)$

$2Cl^-(aq) \rightarrow Cl_2(g) + 2e^-$

$2H^+(aq) + 2e^- \rightarrow H_2(g)$

brine + sodium hydroxide solution

diaphragm

Chlorine gas, Cl_2, is useful for making plastics like poly(chloroethene) (PVC), making synthetic rubber, sterilising water and making bleach.

Brine plus solution of **sodium hydroxide**, which is useful to react with chlorine to make bleach and react with fats and oils to make soap.

This electrolysis process is looked at again under the chlor-alkali industry on page 147.

HOW ARE REACTIVE METALS EXTRACTED?

Many metals are too reactive to be discharged by electrolysis in aqueous solution. For such metals, often the only practicable way to extract them is by melting a suitable metal compound and electrolysing it. Magnesium and sodium are extracted by electrolysing the melted chloride and aluminium is extracted by electrolysis of melted aluminium oxide.

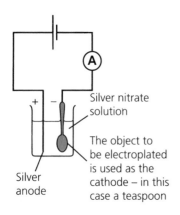

Electroplating involves plating a thin layer of a valuable metal like silver onto a less valuable metal like steel.

WHAT IS ELECTROPLATING?

Electroplating involves using electrolysis to coat an object with a thin film of metal. Often this is done for economic reasons, with a fairly cheap metal like steel being coated with more expensive metals like silver, gold or chromium.

Electroplating can also be used to modify the chemical reactivity of the object plated. One example of this is that steel cans for food containers can be plated with a thin layer of tin inside. Tin itself is too soft and expensive to use for the can, but it is fairly unreactive, and prevents the food from causing the steel to rust.

HOW IS ELECTROLYSIS USED TO PURIFY METALS?

Often at the end of a chemical process the metal extracted is still impure. Copper is needed for precision electrical equipment and works better if it is very pure. Copper can be purified by making a large impure block of copper the anode, and a thin piece of very pure copper the cathode. The two electrodes are then immersed in copper(II) sulphate solution. Copper metal dissolves off the anode and is deposited onto the cathode. However, any impurities either remain in solution or are left behind at the bottom of the container as a 'sludge'.

Purifying metals: impure copper is made into the anode in a bath of copper(II) sulphate. During electrolysis pure copper is deposited on the copper cathode and impurities are left behind.

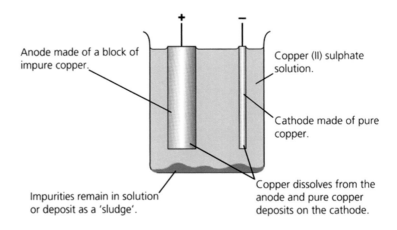

Anode made of a block of impure copper.

Copper (II) sulphate solution.

Cathode made of pure copper.

Impurities remain in solution or deposit as a 'sludge'.

Copper dissolves from the anode and pure copper deposits on the cathode.

Oxidation and reduction

In electrolysis, negative ions give up electrons and usually form molecules (e.g. Cl_2, Br_2), whereas positive ions accept electrons and usually form metallic atoms (e.g. Cu, Al).

The loss of electrons is **oxidation** (the non-metal ions are oxidised), the gain of electrons is **reduction** (the metal ions are reduced).

Evidence for the ionic theory

Electrolysis and the movement of ions in solutions and molten substances provides evidence for the ionic theory.

QUESTIONS

Q1 Explain the following terms:
   a electrolysis
   b electrolyte
   c electrode
   d anode
   e cathode.

Q2 Write half equations for the following reactions:
   a the formation of aluminium atoms from aluminium ions
   b the formation of sodium ions from sodium atoms
   c the formation of oxygen from oxide ions
   d the formation of bromine from bromide ions.

Q3 Zinc bromide $ZnBr_2$ is an ionic solid. Why does the solid not conduct electricity?

Q4 Sodium chloride, NaCl, is ionic. What are the products at the anode and cathode of:
   a solid sodium chloride,
   b aqueous sodium chloride.

Q5 An iron fork is to be sliver plated. Which metal would be the anode and which the cathode?

Q6 Write the half equations for when molten silver iodide is electrolysed.

More questions
on the CD ROM

METALLIC CRYSTALS

Metallic bonding

Metals are giant structures with high melting and boiling points.

Metal atoms give up one or more of their electrons to form positive ions, called **cations**. The electrons they give up form a 'sea of electrons' surrounding the positive metal ions, and the negative electrons are attracted to the positive ions, holding the structure together.

The electrons are free to move through the whole structure, which is why metals conduct electricity. The electrons are **delocalised**, meaning they are not fixed in one position.

The properties of metals

Metals are shiny, malleable (can be hammered into a sheet), ductile (can be drawn into a wire), good conductors of electricity and good conductors of heat.

Metals are good conductors because the electrons are free to move through the structure. When a metal is in an electric circuit, electrons can move toward the positive terminal and the negative terminal can supply electrons into the metal.

Metals are malleable and ductile because metallic bonds are not as rigid as the bonds in diamond, although they are still very strong. So the ions in the metal can move around into different positions when the metal is hammered or worked.

Ions and electrons in a metal.

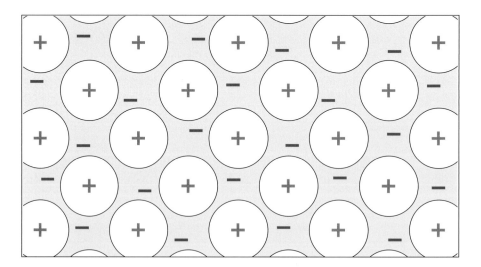

QUESTIONS

Q1 Graphite can conduct electricity in only one plane but metals can conduct in all planes. Explain these facts.

Q2 Use the information in the table to answer the questions that follow.

Substance	Melting point/°C	Boiling point/°C	Solid	Molten
A	751	1244	poor	good
B	−50	148	poor	poor
C	630	1330	good	good
D	247	696	poor	poor

Which substance:
a is a metal
b contains ionic bonds
c has a giant covalent structure
d has a simple molecular structure?

More questions on the CD ROM

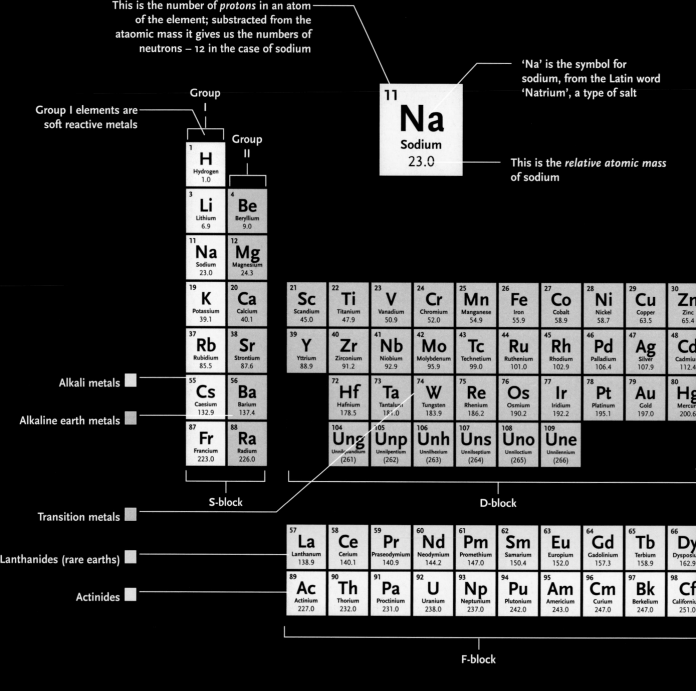

This is the number of *protons* in an atom of the element; substracted from the ataomic mass it gives us the numbers of neutrons – 12 in the case of sodium

'Na' is the symbol for sodium, from the Latin word 'Natrium', a type of salt

11
Na
Sodium
23.0

This is the *relative atomic mass* of sodium

Group I elements are soft reactive metals

Alkali metals

Alkaline earth metals

Transition metals

Lanthanides (rare earths)

Actinides

S-block

D-block

F-block

A map of the chemical world

The first maps of the world were made by Greek and Arab scholars, and have always told us more than simply how to get to where we are going. How far must we travel, how long will it take, and what will we find when we get there? For visitors to a new country or town, a map is the first place to turn to. Chemistry has its own map – the periodic table. All known elements are listed there. From the information given, we can determine their atomic structure, predict which are solid, liquid or gas, and learn much about their properties. In the world of inorganic chemistry, the periodic table is an indispensable guide.

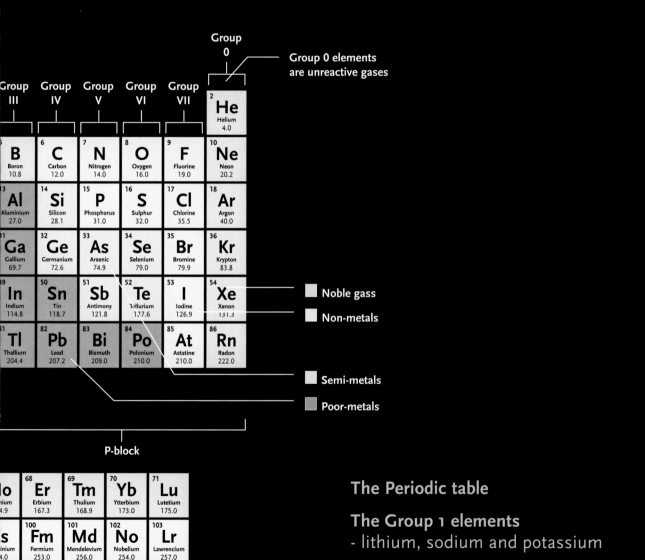

Group
0

Group 0 elements
are unreactive gases

Group III	Group IV	Group V	Group VI	Group VII	
					2 **He** Helium 4.0
5 **B** Boron 10.8	6 **C** Carbon 12.0	7 **N** Nitrogen 14.0	8 **O** Oxygen 16.0	9 **F** Fluorine 19.0	10 **Ne** Neon 20.2
13 **Al** Aluminium 27.0	14 **Si** Silicon 28.1	15 **P** Phosphorus 31.0	16 **S** Sulphur 32.0	17 **Cl** Chlorine 35.5	18 **Ar** Argon 40.0
31 **Ga** Gallium 69.7	32 **Ge** Germanium 72.6	33 **As** Arsenic 74.9	34 **Se** Selenium 79.0	35 **Br** Bromine 79.9	36 **Kr** Krypton 83.8
49 **In** Indium 114.8	50 **Sn** Tin 118.7	51 **Sb** Antimony 121.8	52 **Te** Tellurium 127.6	53 **I** Iodine 126.9	54 **Xe** Xenon 131.3
81 **Tl** Thallium 204.4	82 **Pb** Lead 207.2	83 **Bi** Bismuth 209.0	84 **Po** Polonium 210.0	85 **At** Astatine 210.0	86 **Rn** Radon 222.0

Noble gass

Non-metals

Semi-metals

Poor-metals

P-block

68 **Er** Erbium 167.3	69 **Tm** Thulium 168.9	70 **Yb** Ytterbium 173.0	71 **Lu** Lutetium 175.0
100 **Fm** Fermium 253.0	101 **Md** Mendelevium 256.0	102 **No** Nobelium 254.0	103 **Lr** Lawrencium 257.0

THE PERIODIC TABLE

The arrangement of the periodic table

In the nineteenth century, new elements were being discovered, and chemists were trying to organise the known elements into patterns that related to similarities in their properties. John Dalton first suggested arranging the elements according to their atomic masses, from the lightest to the heaviest.

When the structure of the atom was better known, the elements were arranged in order of increasing atomic number, and then the patterns worked. (Atomic number is the number of protons in the atom.)

How are elements classified in the modern periodic table?

Elements are the building blocks from which all materials are made. Over 100 elements have now been identified, and each element has its own properties and reactions. In the periodic table, elements with similar properties and reactions are put close together.

The periodic table arranges the elements in order of increasing atomic number. The elements are then arranged in periods and groups.

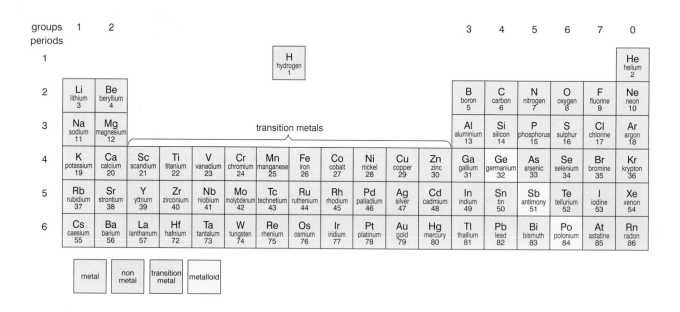

Periods

Rows of elements are arranged in increasing atomic number from left to right. Rows correspond to periods which are numbered from 1 to 7.

Groups

Columns contain elements with the atomic number increasing down the column. They are numbered from 1 to 7 and 0 (group 0 is often referred to as group 8).

Families

Some groups are families of elements – the alkali metals (Group 1), the alkaline earth metals (Group 2) and the halogens (Group 7).

Metals and non-metals

Most elements can be classified as either metals or non-metals. In the periodic table, the metals are arranged on the left and in the middle, and the non-metals are on the right.

Metalloid elements are between metals and non-metals. They have some properties of metals and some of non-metals. Examples of metalloids are antimony and germanium.

Metals and non-metals have quite different physical and chemical properties.

A* EXTRA

- It is important to understand the relationship between group number, number of outer electrons and metallic-nonmetallic character across periods.

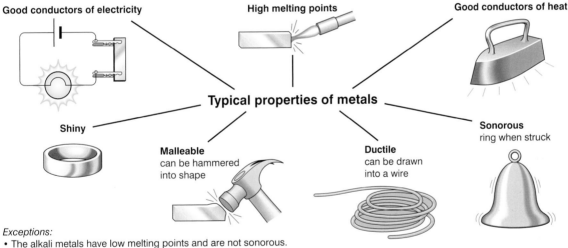

Good conductors of electricity

High melting points

Good conductors of heat

Typical properties of metals

Shiny

Malleable can be hammered into shape

Ductile can be drawn into a wire

Sonorous ring when struck

Exceptions:
- The alkali metals have low melting points and are not sonorous.
- Mercury has a low melting point.

Metals. Clockwise from top left: zinc, silver foil, lead shot, copper crystals.

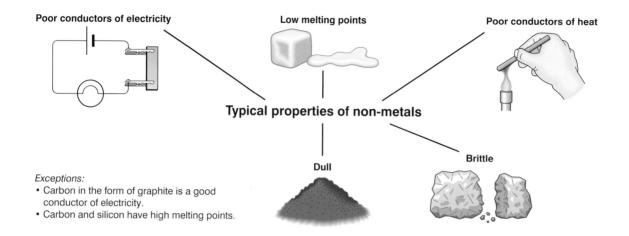

Poor conductors of electricity

Low melting points

Poor conductors of heat

Typical properties of non-metals

Dull

Brittle

Exceptions:
• Carbon in the form of graphite is a good conductor of electricity.
• Carbon and silicon have high melting points.

Non-metals. Clockwise from top left: sulphur, bromine, phosphorus, carbon, iodine.

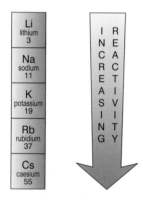

Li	I R
lithium 3	N E
Na	C A
sodium 11	R C
K	E T
potassium 19	A I
Rb	S V
rubidium 37	I I
Cs	N T
caesium 55	G Y

Group 1 elements become more reactive as you go further down the group.

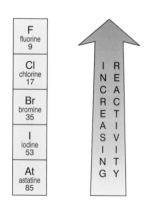

F	I R
fluorine 9	N E
Cl	C A
chlorine 17	R C
Br	E T
bromine 35	A I
I	S V
iodine 53	I I
At	N T
astatine 85	G Y

The Group 7 elements become more reactive as you go further up the group.

Charges on ions and the periodic table

We can explain why elements in the same group have similar reactions in terms of the electron structures of their atoms (see Unit 1). Elements with the same number of electrons in their outer shells have similar chemical properties. The relationship between the group number and the number of electrons in the outer electron shell of the atom is shown in the table

Group number	1	2	3	4	5	6	7	0 (8)
Electrons in the outer electron shell	1	2	3	4	5	6	7	2 or 8 (full)

The ion formed by an element can be worked out from the **position of the element in the periodic table**. The elements in group 4 and group 8 (or 0) generally do not form ions.

Group number	1	2	3	4	5	6	7	8 (or 0)
Ion charge	1+	2+	3+	X	3–	2–	1–	X

Reactivities of elements

As you go from the top to the bottom of the periodic table, metals become more reactive but non-metals become less reactive.

Metallic and non-metallic character

The picture of the periodic table shows the metals and non metals. Most elements are metals.

Metallic character increases down groups in the periodic table. As the atom gets bigger, the outer electrons are further away from the nucleus and so can be removed more easily, as the atoms react to form ions.

QUESTIONS

Q1 Look at the diagram representing the periodic table. The letters stand for elements.

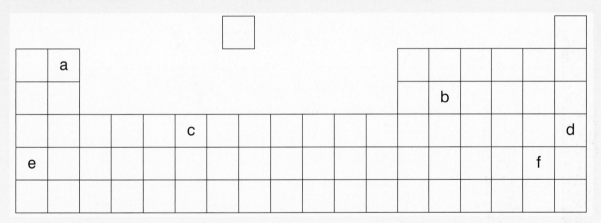

    a Which element is in group 4?
    b Which element is in the second period?
    c Which element is a noble gas?
    d Which element is a transition metal?
    e Which elements are non-metals?
    f Which element is most likely to be a gas?

Q2 Why do elements in the same group react in similar ways?

Q3 In the periodic table, what is the trend in reactivity;
    a down a metallic group?
    b down a non-metallic group?

Q4 In terms of electron transfer in bonding, what is the difference between metallic and non-metallic elements?

Q5 Why are large metal atoms more reactive than smaller atoms in the same group.

More questions on the CD ROM

THE GROUP 1 ELEMENTS – LITHIUM, SODIUM AND POTASSIUM

Reactivity of the group 1 elements

All the Group 1 elements react with water to produce an alkaline solution. This provides a basis for their recognition as a family of elements.

These very reactive metals all have only **one electron** in their outer electron shell. This electron is readily given away when the metal reacts with non-metals. The more electrons a metal atom has to lose in a reaction, the more energy is needed to start the reaction. This is why the group 2 elements are less reactive – they have to lose two electrons when they react.

Reactivity increases down the group because, as the atom gets bigger, the outer electron is further away from the nucleus and so can be removed more easily, as the atoms react and form **cations**.

Properties of group 1 metals

Soft to cut.

Shiny when cut, but quickly tarnish in the air.

Very low melting points compared with most metals.

Very low densities compared with most metals (lithium, sodium and potassium will float on water).

React very easily with air, water and elements such as chlorine. The alkali metals are so reactive that they are stored in oil to prevent reaction with air and water.

Reaction	Observations	Equations
Air or oxygen	The metals burn easily and their compounds colour flames: • lithium – red • sodium – orange/yellow • potassium – lilac A white solid oxide is formed.	lithium + oxygen → lithium oxide $4Li(s) + O_2(g) \rightarrow 2Li_2O(s)$ sodium + oxygen → sodium oxide $4Na(s) + O_2(g) \rightarrow 2Na_2O(s)$ potassium + oxygen → potassium oxide $4K(s) + O_2(g) \rightarrow 2K_2O(s)$

Reaction	Observations	Equations
Water	The metals react vigorously. They float on the surface, moving around rapidly. The heat of the reaction melts the metal so it forms a sphere. Bubbles of gas are given off, and the metal 'disappears'. With the more reactive metals (e.g. potassium) the hydrogen gas produced burns. The resulting solution is alkaline.	lithium + water $\rightarrow$ lithium hydroxide + hydrogen $2Li(s) + 2H_2O(l) \rightarrow 2LiOH(aq) + H_2(g)$ sodium + water $\rightarrow$ sodium hydroxide + hydrogen $2Na(s) + 2H_2O(l) \rightarrow 2NaOH(aq) + H_2(g)$ potassium + water $\rightarrow$ potassium hydroxide + hydrogen $2K(s) + 2H_2O(l) \rightarrow 2KOH(aq) + H_2(g)$
Chlorine sodium chlorine	The metals react easily, burning in the chlorine to form a white solid.	lithium + chlorine $\rightarrow$ lithium chloride $2Li(s) + Cl_2(g) \rightarrow 2LiCl(s)$ sodium + chlorine $\rightarrow$ sodium chloride $2Na(s) + Cl_2(g) \rightarrow 2NaCl(s)$ potassium + chlorine $\rightarrow$ potassium chloride $2K(s) + Cl_2(g) \rightarrow 2KCl(s)$

Thermal decomposition of group 1 nitrates and carbonates

When heated group 1 nitrates decompose.

Lithium nitrate decomposes differently to all the other group 1 nitrates because it produces three products – the oxide, nitrogen dioxide and oxygen.

$$4LiNO_3(s) \rightarrow 2Li_2O(s) + 4NO_2(g) + O_2(g)$$

All the other nitrates only produce the nitrite and oxygen i.e. they do not decompose as much as lithium nitrate, e.g.

$$2NaNO_3(s) \rightarrow 2NaNO_2(s) + O_2(g)$$

Lithium carbonate is the only group 1 carbonate that decomposes when heated in a Bunsen flame, e.g.

$$Li_2CO_3(s) \rightarrow Li_2O(s) + CO_2(g)$$

All other group 1 carbonates are stable at the temperature of a Bunsen flame.

Sodium burning in chlorine.

Compounds of the group 1 metals

The compounds are usually colourless crystals and formed by ionic bonding. This means that the compounds of Group 1 metals are usually soluble in water. Some examples are sodium chloride $NaCl$ and potassium nitrate KNO_3.

The compounds of the alkali metals are widely used:
- lithium carbonate – in light sensitive lenses for glasses
- lithium hydroxide – removes carbon dioxide in air-conditioning systems
- sodium chloride – table salt
- sodium carbonate – a water softener
- sodium hydroxide – used in paper manufacture
- monosodium glutamate – a flavour enhancer
- sodium sulphite – a preservative
- potassium nitrate – a fertiliser; also used in explosives.

QUESTIONS

Q1 This question is about the group 1 elements.
a Which is the most reactive of the elements?
b Why are the elements stored in oil?
c Which element is the easiest to cut?
d Why do the elements tarnish quickly when they are cut?
e Why is the group known as the alkali metals?
f Why does sodium float when added to water?

Q2 Write word equations and symbol equations for the following reactions:
a rubidium and oxygen
b caesium and water
c potassium and chlorine.

Q3 These questions are about lithium.
a In terms of electron transfer, why is lithium classed as a 'metal'?
b Give two reason why lithium is the least reactive group 1 metal.

Q4 Why are the Group 1 metals stored under oil?

Q5 Write balanced chemical equations (including state symbols) for the following reactions:
a burning potassium in oxygen
b adding sodium to water.

More questions on the CD ROM

THE GROUP 2 ELEMENTS – MAGNESIUM AND CALCIUM

Videos & questions on the CD ROM

Reactivity of the Group 2 elements

These metals all have two electrons in their outer shell. The electrons are given away when the metal reacts with non-metals. Because the Group 2 elements have to give two electrons away more energy is needed to start a reaction than with the Group 1 elements. This is why the Group 2 elements are less reactive than the Group 1 elements.

Reactivity increases down the group because as the atom gets bigger, the outer electrons are further away from the nucleus and so can be removed more easily to form ions.

Properties of Group 2 metals

Harder than Group 1 metals

Shiny when cut, but they tarnish fairly quickly in the air because a layer of oxide forms on the cut surface

Higher melting points than Group 1 metals

Higher densities than Group 1 elements

React very easily with air, water and other elements but much less vigorously than the Group 1 elements

Group 2 elements become more reactive as you go further down the group.

Reaction	Observations	Equations
Air or oxygen	The metals burn easily and their compounds colour flames: • calcium – brick-red • strontium – crimson • barium – apple green	magnesium + oxygen → magnesium oxide $2Mg(s) + O_2(g) \rightarrow 2MgO$
Water	They react with water but not so rapidly as Group 1	calcium + water → calcium hydroxide + hydrogen $Ca(s) + 2H_2O(l) \rightarrow Ca(OH)_2(aq) + H_2(g)$

Magnesium burning in chlorine.

Compounds of the Group 2 metals

The compounds are usually white and crystalline. Some examples are magnesium oxide MgO and calcium carbonate $CaCO_3$.

The oxides react with water to form hydroxides. CaO is produced on a large scale to use in cement-making.

The carbonates of Group 2 metals decompose when heated.

e.g. $CaCO_3(s) \rightarrow CaO(s) + CO_2(g)$

All the group 2 nitrates decompose when heated in a Bunsen flame to produce the oxide, nitrogen dioxide and oxygen.

e.g. $2Mg(NO_3)_2 \rightarrow 2MgO(s) + 4NO_2(g) + O_2(g)$

QUESTIONS

Q1 This question is about the Group 2 elements.
  a Which is the most reactive of the elements?
  b Which is the least reactive?
  c What is the reason for this reactivity trend?
  d Why are the metals harder and with a higher melting point than the Group 1 metals?
  e Write word equations and symbol equations for the following reactions:
     i magnesium and oxygen
     ii calcium and water
     iii strontium and fluorine

Q2 How does reactivity change down the Group 2 metals?

Q3 Why are the Group 2 metals less reactive than Group 1 metals?

More questions on the CD ROM

THE GROUP 7 ELEMENTS –
CHLORINE, BROMINE AND IODINE

Videos & questions
on the CD ROM

Group 7 – The halogens

The term 'halogen' means 'salt-maker' and the halogens react with most metals to make salts.

The halogen elements have **seven electrons in their outermost electron shell**, so they only need to gain one electron to obtain a full outer electron shell, which makes them **very reactive**. The halogens react with metals, gaining an electron and forming a singly charged negative ion (see ionic bonding).

The reactivity of the elements **decreases down the group** because, as the atom gets bigger, an eighth electron will be further from the attractive force of the nucleus. This means it is harder for the atom to gain this electron.

At room temperature and atmospheric pressure, chlorine is a pale green gas, bromine an orange liquid and iodine is a dark purple solid.

Differences between the Group 7 elements

Appearance: fluorine is a pale yellow gas; chlorine is a yellow-green gas; bromine is a brown liquid; iodine is a black shiny solid.

Similarities between the Group 7 elements

All have **7 electrons** in their outermost electron shell.

All exist as **diatomic** molecules (molecules containing two atoms – e.g. F_2, Cl_2, Br_2, I_2).

Halogens react with water and react with metals to form **salts**.

Iodine has very low solubility and little reaction with water. The reaction of I_2 + Fe is very slow.

They undergo **displacement** reactions.

Reaction	Observations	Equations
Water chlorine gas → water	The halogens dissolve in water and also react with it, forming solutions that behave as bleaches. Chlorine solution is pale yellow. Bromine solution is orange/brown. Iodine solution is brown.	chlorine + water → hydrochloric acid + chloric(I) acid $Cl_2(g) + H_2O(l) \rightarrow HCl(aq) + HClO(aq)$
Metals chlorine iron wool	The halogens will form salts with all metals. For example, gold leaf will catch fire in chlorine without heating. With a metal such as iron, brown fumes of iron(III) chloride form.	iron + chlorine → iron(III) chloride $2Fe(s) + 3Cl_2(g) \rightarrow 2FeCl_3(s)$ Fluor*ine* forms salts called fluor*ides*. Chlor*ine* forms salts called chlor*ides*. Brom*ine* forms salts called brom*ides*. Iod*ine* forms salts called iod*ides*.

Reaction	Observations	Equations
Displacement	A more reactive halogen will displace a less reactive halogen from a solution of a salt.	
chlorine gas	Chlorine displaces bromine from sodium bromide solution. The colourless solution (sodium bromide) will turn brown as the chlorine is added due to the formation of bromine.	chlorine + sodium bromide $\rightarrow$ sodium chloride + bromine $Cl_2(g) + 2NaBr(aq) \rightarrow 2NaCl(aq) + Br_2(aq)$
potassium iodide solution iodine being formed	Chlorine displaces iodine from sodium iodide solution. The colourless solution (sodium iodide) will turn brown as the chlorine is added due to the formation of iodine.	chlorine + sodium iodide $\rightarrow$ sodium chloride + iodine $Cl_2(g) + 2NaI(aq) \rightarrow 2NaCl(aq) + I_2(aq)$

Uses of halogens

The halogens and their compounds have a wide range of uses:

- fluorides – in toothpaste help to prevent tooth decay
- fluorine compounds – make plastics like Teflon (the non-stick surface on pans)
- chlorofluorocarbons – propellants in aerosols and refrigerants (now being phased out due to their effect on the ozone layer)
- chlorine – a bleach
- chlorine compounds – kill bacteria in drinking water and are used in antiseptics
- hydrochloric acid – widely used in industry
- bromine compounds – make pesticides
- silver bromide – the light sensitive film coating on photographic film
- iodine solution – an antiseptic.

Hydrogen chloride and hydrochloric acid

Hydrogen chloride is a very important molecular compound formed from the reaction of hydrogen and chlorine:

hydrogen + chlorine $\rightarrow$ hydrogen chloride
$$H_2(g) + Cl_2(g) \rightarrow 2HCl(g)$$

When hydrogen chloride is dissolved in water it forms hydrochloric acid
hydrogen chloride + water $\rightarrow$ hydrochloric acid

$$HCl(g) + H_2O(l) \rightarrow H_3O^+ + Cl^-$$

However, a solution of hydrogen chloride in methylbenzene contains HCl molecules in solution. The HCl does not **dissociate** into ions. HCl in methylbenzene does not behave as a typical acid as HCl(aq) does. It also has a low electrical conductivity because no ions are present.

Ammonia gas and hydrogen chloride gas react to form a white smoke of ammonium chloride (a test either for ammonia or for hydrogen chloride).

The laboratory preparation of chlorine from hydrochloric acid

The most common method is to heat concentrated hydrochloric acid with manganese dioxide as shown in the diagram below.

manganese dioxide + hydrochloric acid → chlorine + manganese chloride + water

$$MnO_2 + 4HCl \rightarrow MnCl_2 + 2H_2O + Cl_2$$

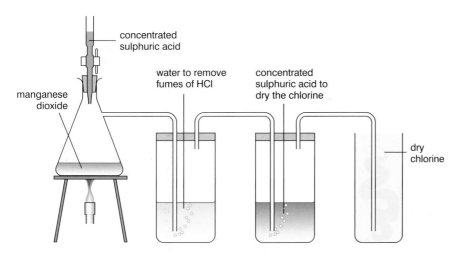

To test for chlorine hold a piece of damp indicator paper in the gas and chlorine will bleach it white.

In the laboratory a clean dry sample of chlorine can be made by adding concentrated hydrochloric acid to potassium manganate (VII).

The equation for the reaction is:

$$2KMnO_4(s) + 16HCl(aq) \rightarrow 2KCl(aq) + 5Cl_2(g) + 2MnCl_2(aq) + 8H_2O(aq)$$

QUESTIONS

Q1 This question is about the Group 7 elements.
   a Which is the most reactive of the elements?
   b Which of the elements exists as a liquid at room temperature and pressure?
   c Which of the elements exists as a solid at room temperature and pressure?
   d Why are halogens such reactive elements?

Q2 Write word and symbol equations for the following reactions:
   a sodium and chlorine
   b magnesium and bromine
   c hydrogen and fluorine.

Q3 Write a word equation and symbol equation for the reaction between bromine and sodium iodide.

Q4 Explain why reactivity increases as you go up Group 7.

More questions on the CD ROM

OXYGEN AND OXIDES

Videos & questions on the CD ROM

The gases in the air

These are the main gases found in normal, dry air and their approximate percentage by volume. Air will also contain small quantities of the other noble gases: neon, helium, krypton and xenon, and it may also contain water vapour.

Nitrogen	Oxygen	Argon	Carbon dioxide
78.1%	21.0%	0.9%	trace

The industrial extraction of oxygen, from liquid air

Oxygen, nitrogen and the noble gases are all obtained from air. The air is liquified and the gases are separated by fractional distillation.

The industrial process has several stages
1. Carbon dioxide and water are removed. The air is cooled to about -80°C so that water and carbon dioxide solidify and can be removed.
2. The air is cooled and compressed.
3. The air is allowed to expand quickly, this cools the air still further.
4. The air is now at about -200°C and at this temperature it liquifies.
5. The liquid air is fractionally distilled. The gasses can be separated because they have different boiling points: oxygen (-183°C), nitrogen (-196°C).

The reactions of oxygen in the air

Magnesium burning in oxygen.

The **oxides** of elements can often be made by heating the element in air or oxygen. For example, the metal magnesium burns in oxygen to form magnesium oxide:

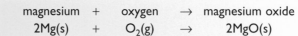

$$\text{magnesium} + \text{oxygen} \rightarrow \text{magnesium oxide}$$
$$2Mg(s) + O_2(g) \rightarrow 2MgO(s)$$

Magnesium oxide forms as a white powder. When distilled water is added to the powder and the mixture is tested with universal indicator, the pH is greater than 7 – the oxide has formed an **alkaline** solution.

When sulphur is burnt in oxygen, sulphur dioxide gas is formed:

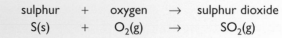

$$\text{sulphur} + \text{oxygen} \rightarrow \text{sulphur dioxide}$$
$$S(s) + O_2(g) \rightarrow SO_2(g)$$

When this is dissolved in water and then tested with universal indicator solution, the pH is less than 7 – the oxide has formed an **acidic** solution.

The oxides of most elements can be classified as **basic oxides** or **acidic oxides**. Some elements form **neutral oxides**. For example, water is a neutral oxide. Basic oxides that dissolve in water are called **alkalis**.

Sulphur burns in oxygen with a blue flame to give a colourless gas.

Bases and alkalis react with acids to form salts in reactions known as **neutralisation** reactions. A typical neutralisation reaction occurs when sodium hydroxide (an alkali) reacts with hydrochloric acid. The salt formed is sodium chloride, common salt:

alkali	+	acid	$\rightarrow$	salt	+	water
sodium hydroxide	+	hydrochloric acid	$\rightarrow$	sodium chloride	+	water
$NaOH(aq)$	+	$HCl(aq)$	$\rightarrow$	$NaCl(aq)$	+	$H_2O(l)$

Iron will burn in air and react with oxygen if it is in powder or wire form. A black oxide forms.

iron	+	oxygen	$\rightarrow$	iron oxide
$3Fe(s)$	+	$2O_2(g)$	$\rightarrow$	$Fe_3O_4(g)$

Copper reacts slowly with oxygen, it will go gradually darker on heating and also makes a black oxide.

copper	+	oxygen	$\rightarrow$	copper oxide
$2Cu(s)$	+	O_2	$\rightarrow$	$2CuO(s)$

Charcoal is mainly carbon. It burns to give carbon dioxide.

Methane. When a hydrocarbon is burnt in a plentiful supply of air it reacts with the oxygen in the air (it is **oxidised**) to form carbon dioxide and water. This reaction is an example of **combustion**.

hydrocarbon	+	oxygen	$\rightarrow$	carbon dioxide	+	water

For example, when methane (natural gas) is burnt:

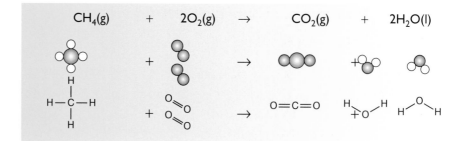

The complete combustion of methane in a plentiful supply of air.

The incomplete combustion of methane produces carbon or carbon monoxide. See page 138 for more detail about this process and the problems it causes the environment.

Oxidation and reduction

A chemical reaction where there is addition of oxygen is called **oxidation**. An example is combustion in air. A chemical reaction where oxygen is removed is called **reduction**.

To determine the percentage by volume of oxygen in the air

Here is a simple experiment to show the percentage of the oxygen in the air.

Experiment to show the percentage of oxygen in the air.

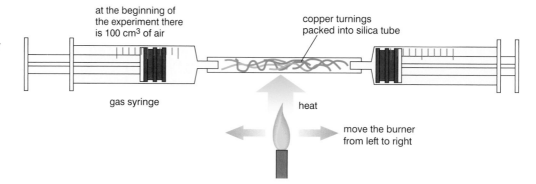

At the beginning, the experiment contains 100 cm³ of air. In the experiment the gas is continually being passed from one syringe to the other over the copper in the silica tube. When the copper is heated the amount of gas gradually decreases as the oxygen in the air is used up. The copper reacts with the oxygen in the air to form copper oxide (see the equation above).

Eventually the gas volume stops contracting as all the oxygen has been used up. The volume of gas in the syringes goes down to about 79 cm³ showing that about 21 cm³ of the air was oxygen.

The percentage of oxygen in the air is 21% on average but this does vary by a small amount depending on the part of the world where the experiment is performed.

Sulphur dioxide

Sulphur dioxide is formed when sulphur is burnt in oxygen.

It reacts with water to form **sulphurous acid.**

sulphur dioxide + water → sulphurous acid

$$SO_2 + H_2O → H_2SO_3$$

In the atmosphere, sulphur dioxide, which is a waste product from burning petrol in a car, can react with oxygen.

sulphur dioxide + oxygen + water → sulphuric acid + water

$$2SO_2(g) + O_2(g) + 2H_2O(l) → H_2SO_4(aq) + H_2O(l)$$

This is one of the processes that makes acid rain.

Sulphur dioxide reacts with alkalis to form salts.

Carbon dioxide

Carbon dioxide is an important gas. It can be made in the laboratory by the reaction of dilute hydrochloric acid and calcium carbonate, in the form of marble chips.

calcium carbonate + hydrochloric acid → carbon dioxide + water + calcium chloride

$$CaCO_3(s) + 2HCl(aq) → CO_2 + H_2O + CaCl_2(aq)$$

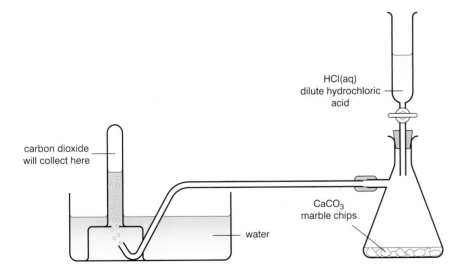

The laboratory preparation of carbon dioxide gas.

HCl(aq) dilute hydrochloric acid

carbon dioxide will collect here

$CaCO_3$ marble chips

water

The gas can be dried by bubbling it through concentrated sulphuric acid.

If the gas is bubbled through limewater (calcium hydroxide solution), a white precipitate forms. This is used as a laboratory test for carbon dioxide.

The properties and reactions of carbon dioxide

Carbon dioxide is a colourless gas which is more dense than air. It becomes solid below -78°C. This is called **dry ice**.

Carbon dioxide dissolves slightly in water. It also reacts with water to form **carbonic acid**.

water + carbon dioxide ⇌ carbonic acid

$$H_2O(l) + CO_2(g) \rightleftharpoons H_2CO_3(aq)$$

Carbon dioxide reacts with alkalis in solution to form salts called **carbonates**. Here is the reaction with sodium hydroxide solution.

carbon dioxide + sodium hydroxide → sodium carbonate + water

$$CO_2(g) + 2NaOH(aq) \rightarrow Na_2CO_3 + H_2O$$

Carbon dioxide reacts with limewater (calcium hydroxide solution) to form a cloudy white precipitate of insoluble calcium carbonate. If carbon dioxide continues to be passed through, the cloudiness disappears, as the calcium carbonate is changed into calcium hydrogencarbonate, which is soluble.

carbon dioxide + calcium hydroxide → calcium carbonate + water

$$CO_2(g) + Ca(OH)_2(aq) \rightarrow CaCO_3(s) + H_2O(l)$$

calcium carbonate + water + carbon dioxide → calcium hydrogencarbonate

$$CaCO_3(s) + H_2O(l) + CO_2(g) \rightarrow Ca(HCO_3)_2(aq)$$

The uses of carbon dioxide

Carbon dioxide is used for make fizzy (carbonated) drinks such as sodas and mineral waters. It is added to the drinks under pressure so that it dissolves in the liquid and then fizzes out (comes out of solution) when the bottle or can is opened and the pressure is released.

Carbon dioxide is also used in fire extinguishers. Because it is denser than air it settles around the fire and keeps the oxygen of the air away from the fire. As carbon dioxide does not burn, the fire is put out.

The reaction of nitrogen with oxygen

Nitrogen is usually a very unreactive gas. It does not normally react with oxygen in the air to form oxides. However, under certain special circumstances it can react with oxygen to form nitrogen monoxide and then nitrogen dioxide. Lightning in thunderstorms can release enough energy for these reactions to take place. Also, car engines can generate a high enough temperature and pressure to make the reactions happen.

nitrogen + oxygen → nitrogen monoxide

$$N_2(g) + O_2(g) \rightarrow 2NO(g)$$

nitrogen monoxide + oxygen → nitrogen dioxide

$$2NO(g) + O_2(g) \rightarrow 2NO_2(g)$$

The oxides of nitrogen, along with sulphur dioxide, SO_2, dissolve in rain water in the atmosphere. This then becomes 'acid rain' that affects forests, aquatic life and buildings.

The rusting of iron

Iron can corrode, which means it can be broken down chemically and decay. The corrosion of iron is called rusting and it is a chemical reaction between iron, water and oxygen. A flaky orange solid forms on the surface of the iron.

Water and oxygen from the air must both be present for iron to rust. The rate of rusting will increase if there are electrolytes such as sodium chloride in the water, for example in sea water.

Rusting of iron and mild steel can be prevented by grease, oil, paint, plastic and galvanising, in which a coating of zinc on the surface of the iron protects it from rusting. The zinc corrodes instead of the iron, if the coating is damaged. This is called sacrificial protection. All these methods of rust prevention prevent water and air coming into contact with the surface of the iron.

The reduction of oxides

The reduction of oxides back to the metal depends on the reactivity of the elements involved. If metal oxides are heated with carbon they will be reduced if the metal is less reactive than carbon. Zinc, iron, tin, lead and copper oxides can all be reduced by heating with carbon, because they are less reactive than carbon. However, aluminium, magnesium, calcium, sodium and potassium cannot be reduced by carbon because they are all more reactive than carbon.

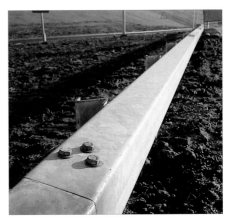

Galvanized iron does not rust as fast as iron on its own. The coating of zinc corrodes in preference to the iron, in the course of which it forms a further protective layer over the iron

QUESTIONS

Q1 Which method is used to obtain oxygen from the air?

Q2 What is the cause of rusting of iron?

Q3 An iron nail is coated with a layer of zinc to stop it rusting.
a What is this called?
b Explain how zinc protects the iron from rusting.

Q4 Write the balanced chemical equation for the reaction of sodium oxide with water.

More questions on the CD ROM

SULPHUR

About two-thirds of the sulphur found in the atmosphere comes from sulphurous gases emitted by volcanoes.

The allotropes of sulphur

Sulphur is found in many places in the world, and is often released by volcanoes. Many elements form compounds with sulphur which are called sulphides.

Different forms of the same element are called allotropes. Sulphur exists in three main forms.

RHOMBIC SULPHUR

Rhombic sulphur is sulphur that occurs in rhombus-shaped crystals. The individual molecules are in rings of 8 atoms.

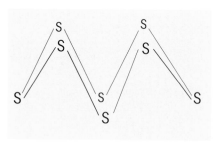

Sulphur in the form of the S_8 molecule.

MONOCLINIC SULPHUR

This occurs if rhombic sulphur is heated up and then cooled. Monoclinic sulphur is in the form of long needle-shaped crystals. The sulphur is still in S_8 molecules but they are arranged into a different crystal structure than rhombic sulphur. The crystals will gradually change back into the rhombic form.

PLASTIC SULPHUR

This can be made if sulphur is heated until it melts and then poured suddenly into cold water. It makes a flexible brown filament. Because the sulphur is cooled suddenly crystals cannot form. If the plastic sulphur is left for a few days it sets hard and it will turn back into rhombic sulphur.

Sulphites and their reactions with dilute acid

When sulphur dioxide is dissolved in water it forms sulphurous acid, H_2SO_3. Salts of sulphurous acids are called sulphites. When sulphites react with dilute acid, sulphur dioxide gas is released. For example:

potassium sulphite + nitric acid $\rightarrow$ sulphur dioxide + potassium nitrite + water

$$K_2SO_3(s) \quad + 2HNO_3(aq) \rightarrow \quad SO_2(g) \quad + \quad 2KNO_3 \quad + H_2O(l)$$

QUESTIONS

Q1 Give two uses for sulphur dioxide.

Q2 Describe the test for sulphites.

More questions on the CD ROM

NITROGEN AND AMMONIA

Videos & questions on the CD ROM

Nitrogen is obtained by the fractional distillation of liquid air.

The uses of nitrogen

Nitrogen is a very inert gas, i.e. it is very unreactive. It is used in the packaging of food to provide a protective atmosphere around the food. Because the food is only in contact with nitrogen and not oxygen, it is protected from oxidation and so can be preserved for a long time.

Ammonia

Ammonia is the most important compound of nitrogen. It is used in the manufacture of fertilisers. It is made industrially by the Haber process. Ammonia is the only common alkaline gas.

Ammonium nitrate fertiliser being sprayed onto a field.

The laboratory preparation of ammonia

In the laboratory, ammonia can be prepared by carefully heating together ammonium chloride and calcium hydroxide. The gas evolved is then passed through solid calcium oxide to dry it. The gas is lighter than air so it is collected by upward delivery. The gas can be tested by putting in a piece of moist red litmus paper. The gas will turn the paper blue, showing that it is alkaline.

ammonium chloride + calcium hydroxide $\rightarrow$ ammonia + water + calcium chloride

$$2NH_4Cl \quad + \quad Ca(OH)_2 \quad \rightarrow \quad 2NH_3 + 2H_2O + \quad CaCl_2$$

The properties of ammonia

Ammonia is a colourless gas that is less dense (lighter) than air. It is very soluble in water. It is the only common alkaline gas.

The chemistry of aqueous ammonia

Ammonia gas is **very soluble** in water where it forms the ammonium ion and the hydroxide ion:

ammonia	+	water	→	ammonium ion	+	hydroxide ion
$NH_3(g)$	+	$H_2O(l)$	→	$NH_4^+(aq)$	+	$OH^-(aq)$

This solution is alkaline, so when UI paper or red litmus paper is added to it, they both change to blue. This is not the test for ammonium ions – any alkaline solution will give this result.

The **test** for the **ammonium ion** is as in the diagram.

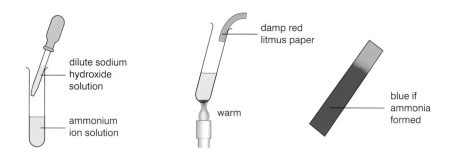

Ammonium salts

Ammonia solution will react with acids to form salts. For example:

ammonia solution	+	dilute sulphuric acid	→	ammonium sulphate
$2NH_3(aq)$	+	$H_2SO_4(aq)$	→	$(NH_4)_2SO_4(aq)$

In a similar way, reaction with dilute nitric acid gives ammonium nitrate and with dilute sulphuric acid give ammonium sulphate.

All these ammonium salts will react with a base to produce ammonia gas. An example is the reaction of ammonium chloride with calcium hydroxide to produce ammonia in the laboratory.

QUESTIONS

Q1 How is nitrogen obtained on an industrial scale?

Q2 An early name for nitrogen was 'azote' meaning 'without life'.
   a Why did the early chemists call nitrogen 'azote'?
   b Give two uses for nitrogen in industry.
   c Nitrogen is diatomic molecule. What does this mean?

More questions on the CD ROM

Q3 How is ammonium sulphate tested to show the presence of the ammonium ion?

HYDROGEN

Videos & questions
on the CD ROM

The effect of dilute acids on metals

There is a general reaction between metals and acids that produces hydrogen.

metal + acid → hydrogen + a salt

The vigour of the reaction depend on the reactivity of the metal.

Here are four metals in order of reactivity: magnesium, aluminium, zinc and iron. Magnesium reacts very quickly with dilute hydrochloric or dilute sulphuric acid, whereas iron reacts well, but not as quickly as magnesium.

The salts are named from the acid, so hydrochloric acid forms chlorides and sulphuric acid forms sulphates.

The laboratory preparation of hydrogen

In the laboratory, hydrogen is usually prepared by the reaction of dilute hydrochloric acid on zinc.

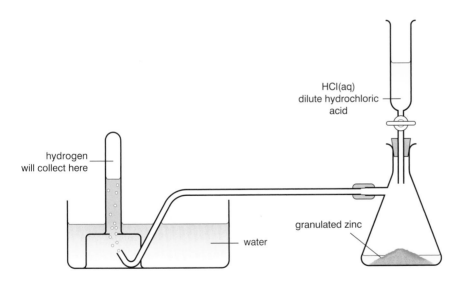

HCl(aq)
dilute hydrochloric
acid

Hydrogen is lighter than air and can be collected over water.

hydrogen will collect here

granulated zinc

water

The combustion of hydrogen with oxygen to form water

A small amount of hydrogen can be tested with a lighted splint. The hydrogen burns in oxygen and makes a 'pop' sound.

On a larger scale it is possible to burn a jet of hydrogen and bring it close to a cold surface. Water condenses on the surface. This is hydrogen oxide.

hydrogen   +   oxygen   →   water

$2H_2(g)$ + $O_2(g)$ → $2H_2O(l)$

A simple chemical test for water

Water turns anhydrous copper sulphate, a white powder, blue. When anhydrous copper sulphate meets water, water of crystallisation is added, and this makes blue crystals.

$$CuSO_4(s) \ + \ 5H_2O(l) \ \rightarrow \ CuSO_4.5H_2O(s)$$

This test will always show the presence of water, but it will not show if the water is pure.

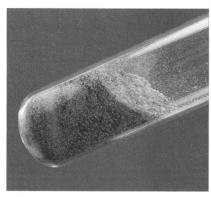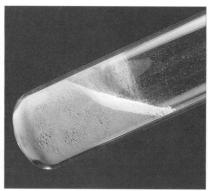

When copper(II) sulphate crystals are heated they turn from blue to white.   The reaction can then be reversed by adding water.

A physical test to show if water is pure

To test if water is pure, we need to test its boiling point with an accurate thermometer. For example, pure water has a boiling point of 100°C but a solution of calcium chloride in water has a boiling point of 102°C.

This can be investigated using a test-tube and a thermometer to measure the boiling point.

The reaction of hydrogen with chlorine

All the halogens react with hydrogen to produce hydrogen halides.

Hydrogen reacts with chlorine when heated, and in sunlight, or ultraviolet light, there can be an explosion.

The basic reaction is:

$$H_2(g) \ + \ Cl_2(g) \ \rightarrow \ 2HCl(g)$$

QUESTIONS

Q1 Describe the test for hydrogen gas.

Q2 The reaction between hydrogen and oxygen is very exothermic. Write the balanced chemical equation (including state symbols) for the reaction.

Q3 Cars can be converted to run on liquid hydrogen as a fuel. Give one advantage and one disadvantage of using liquid hydrogen as a fuel instead of petrol.

More questions on the CD ROM

THE TRANSITION METALS –
IRON AND COPPER

The transition metals

The transition metals are listed in the centre of the periodic table.

All the transition metals have **more than one electron in their outer electron shell**, which is why they are much less reactive than the alkali metals and so are more 'everyday' metals. They have much higher melting points and densities. They react much more slowly with water and with oxygen. Some, like iron, will react with dilute acids – others, like copper, show no reaction. Iron, cobalt and nickel are the only magnetic elements.

They are widely used as construction metals (particularly iron), and they are frequently used as **catalysts** in the chemical industry.

Property	Group I metal	Transition metal
Melting point	low	high
Density	low	high
Colours of compounds	white	coloured
Reactions with water/air	vigorous	slow or no reaction
Reactions with acid	violent (dangerous)	slow or no reaction

The **compounds** of the transition metals are usually **coloured**. Copper compounds are usually blue or green; iron compounds tend to be either green or brown. When sodium hydroxide solution is added to the solution of a transition metal compound, a precipitate of the metal hydroxide is formed. The colour of the precipitate will help to identify the metal. For example:

copper sulphate	+	sodium hydroxide	→	copper(II) hydroxide	+	sodium sulphate
$CuSO_4(aq)$	+	$2NaOH(aq)$	→	$Cu(OH)_2(s)$	+	$Na_2SO_4(aq)$

This can be written as an ionic equation:

$$Cu^{2+}(aq) + 2OH^-(aq) \rightarrow Cu(OH)_2(s)$$

Colour of metal hydroxide	Likely ion present
blue	copper (II) Cu^{2+}
green	nickel (II) Ni^{2+}
green	iron (II) Fe^{2+}
orange/brown	iron (III) Fe^{3+}

The action of steam, hydrogen chloride and chlorine on iron

STEAM

Iron reacts very slowly with water but will react quickly with steam.

iron	+	steam	→	iron oxide	+	hydrogen
$3Fe(s)$	+	$4H_2O(g)$	→	Fe_3O_4	+	$4H_2(g)$

HYDROGEN CHLORIDE

With hydrogen chloride, iron(II) chloride and hydrogen are produced.

iron	+	hydrogen chloride	→	iron(II) chloride	+	hydrogen
$Fe(s)$	+	$2HCl(g)$	→	$FeCl_2(s)$	+	$H_2(g)$

CHLORINE

When iron and chlorine react brown fumes of iron(III) chloride form.

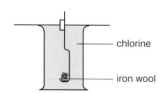
chlorine

iron wool

iron	+	chlorine	→	iron(III) chloride
$2Fe(s)$	+	$3Cl_2(g)$	→	$2FeCl_3(s)$

The formation of iron(II) and iron(III) hydroxides from salt solutions

Iron can form two different hydroxides, iron(II) and iron(III) hydroxides. These are produced from solutions of the salts of iron, for example.

iron(II) sulphate + sodium hydroxide → iron(II) hydroxide + sodium sulphate

$FeSO_4(aq)$	+	$2NaOH(aq)$	→	$Fe(OH)_2(s)$	+	$Na_2SO_4(aq)$

iron(III)chloride + sodium hydroxide → iron(III) hydroxide + sodium chloride

$FeCl_3(aq)$	+	$3NaOH(aq)$	→	$Fe(OH)_3(s)$	+	$3NaCl(aq)$

These experiments can be carried out in the laboratory. The iron hydroxides precipitate out of the solutions.

The iron(II) hydroxide is white when it is pure but often appears to be a pale green colour. Iron(III) hydroxide is an orangey-brown colour.

The redox reaction of concentrated nitric acid on copper

Copper is a very unreactive metal. It does not react with dilute acids but it does react with concentrated nitric acid. The reaction produces brown fumes of nitrogen dioxide.

copper + conc. nitric acid → copper(II) nitrate + water + nitrogen dioxide

Cu	+	$4HNO_3$	→	$Cu(NO_3)_2$	+	$2H_2O$ +	$4NO_2$

This is called a **redox reaction** because there is reduction and oxidation. Nitric acid is reduced and copper is oxidised.

The properties of copper compounds

Copper is a transition metal, and the compounds of transition metals are usually coloured. Copper compounds are usually green or blue.

When sodium hydroxide solution is added to the solution of a transition metal compound, a precipitate of the metal hydroxide is formed. The colour of the precipitate helps to identify the metal. For example

copper sulphate + sodium hydroxide → copper(II) hydroxide + sodium sulphate

$$CuSO_4(aq) + 2NaOH(aq) → Cu(OH)_2(s) + Na_2SO_4(aq)$$

Copper(II) oxide is made when copper is heated. It is a black compound.

copper + oxygen → copper(II)oxide

$$2Cu(s) + O_2(g) → 2CuO(s)$$

When copper(II) oxide reacts with dilute acids, solutions of salts are produced.

copper(II) oxide + hydrochloric acid → copper(II) chloride + water

$$CuO(s) + 2HCl(aq) → CuCl_2(aq) + H_2O(l)$$

copper(II) chloride gives a green solution.

copper(II)oxide + nitric acid → copper(II)nitrate + water

$$CuO(s) + 2HNO_3(aq) → Cu(NO_3)_2(aq) + H_2O(l)$$

copper(II) nitrate gives a blue solution.

copper(II)oxide + sulphuric acid → copper sulphate + water

$$CuO(s) + H_2SO_4(aq) → CuSO_4(aq) + H_2O(l)$$

Copper sulphate is an intense blue colour. If it is heated gently it will turn into a white powder. This is anhydrous copper sulphate. If water is added it will turn blue, this is a test for water.

Some copper compounds decompose on heating.
Copper carbonate decomposes to copper oxide and carbon dioxide.

$$CuCO_3(s) → CuO(s) + CO_2(g)$$

Copper nitrate decomposes and releases nitrogen dioxide and oxygen.

$$2Cu(NO_3)_2(s) → 2CuO(s) + 4NO_2(g) + O_2(g)$$

Copper(I) compounds

The important compounds of copper are copper(II) compounds, but copper can also form copper(I) compounds. Copper(I) oxide is a red-brown colour. It has the formula Cu_2O.

The reaction of copper(II) ions with ammonia

Copper(II) ions, such as copper sulphate solution will react with alkalis. With an ammonia solution it will form copper(II) hydroxide, which is a blue-green precipitate. If more ammonia solution is added, the precipitate will dissolve to form a deep blue solution. A **complex ion** is produced, which contains copper, ammonia and water.

The formula of the complex ion is:

$$[Cu(H_2O)_2(NH_3)_4]^{2+}$$

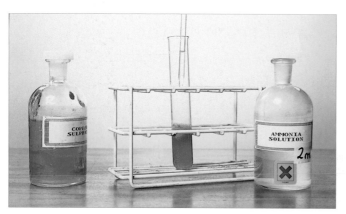

When concentrated ammonia solution is added dropwise to aqueous copper(II) ions, a precipitate of copper(II) hydroxide forms.

On the further addition of excess ammonia solution, the precipitate dissolves as the soluble ammine complex is formed.

Summary of transition metal properties

Copper and iron are typical transition metals. Transition metals all have these typical properties:
- variable valency
- formation of coloured compounds
- formation of complex ions.

QUESTIONS

Q1 Write the balanced chemical equations (including state symbols) for the following reactions:
   a iron and chlorine
   b iron and hydrogen chloride

Q2 Dilute sodium hydroxide solution is added to an aqueous solution of iron (II) sulphate.
   a What is observed when the two solutions are first mixed?
   b What happens, and why, if the mixture is left exposed to the air for some time?

More questions on the CD ROM

Q3 Give two uses of copper.

REACTIVITY SERIES

The order of chemical reactivity

Elements can be arranged in order of their reactivity. The more reactive a metal is, the easier it is to form their compounds and the harder it is to break down their compounds. By looking at the reactivity series we can predict how metals might react.

Chemical reactions and a reactivity series

The pattern in the reactions of an element can be related to the reactivity series.

For example, in the reactions to extract metals from their ores (page 128) the elements that are below carbon in the reactivity series can be obtained by heating their oxides with carbon.

This is called a displacement reaction. The more reactive element, carbon, pushes the less reactive metal, such as iron, out of its compound.

In fact, any element higher up the reactivity series can displace an element lower down the series.

For example, magnesium is higher up the reactivity series than copper. So if magnesium powder is heated with copper oxide then copper and magnesium oxide are produced.

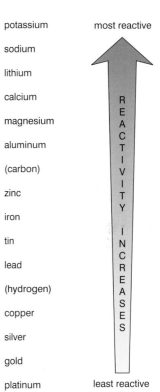

	most reactive
potassium	
sodium	
lithium	
calcium	
magnesium	R
aluminum	E
(carbon)	A
	C
zinc	T
	I
iron	V
	I
tin	T
	Y
lead	
	I
(hydrogen)	N
	C
copper	R
	E
silver	A
	S
gold	E
	S
platinum	least reactive

> magnesium + copper(II) oxide → magnesium oxide + copper
>
> Mg(s) + CuO(s) → MgO(s) + Cu(s)

Your teacher may show you this experiment.

What will happen if copper is heated with magnesium oxide? Nothing happens because copper is lower in the reactivity series than magnesium.

Many such experiments could be carried out to establish the reactivity series.

Here is the reactivity series. It shows elements, mainly metals, in order of decreasing reactivity.

Using displacement reactions to establish a reactivity series

Displacement reactions of metals and their compounds in aqueous solution cam be used to work out the reactivity series.

In the same way that a more reactive element can push a less reactive element out of a compound, a more reactive metal ion in aqueous solution can displace a less reactive one.

For example, if you add zinc to copper(II) sulphate solution the zinc will displace the copper because zinc is a more reactive metal than copper. When the experiment is carried out, the blue colour of the copper ion will fade as copper is produced and zinc ions are made.

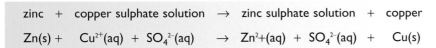

> zinc + copper sulphate solution → zinc sulphate solution + copper
>
> $Zn(s) + Cu^{2+}(aq) + SO_4^{2-}(aq) \rightarrow Zn^{2+}(aq) + SO_4^{2-}(aq) + Cu(s)$

To build up a whole reactivity series, a set of reactions can be tried to see whether metals can displace metal ions, following the general rule that a more reactive metal can displace a less reactive metal.

For example, you may have seen the reaction of copper wire with silver nitrate solution. As the reaction proceeds a shiny grey precipitate appears (this is silver) and the solution begins to turn blue as Cu(II) ions are produced from the copper.

$$copper \ + \ silver \ nitrate \ \rightarrow \ copper \ nitrate \ + \ silver$$
$$Cu(s) \ + \ 2AgNO_3(aq) \ \rightarrow \ Cu(NO_3)_2(aq) \ + \ 2Ag(s)$$

This shows that silver can be displaced by copper and so silver is below copper in the reactivity series

The sacrificial protection of iron and mild steel

The rusting of iron can be prevented by using what we know about the reactivity series.

Zinc is above iron in the reactivity series, i.e. zinc will react more readily than iron.

Galvanised iron is iron which is coated with a layer of zinc. To begin with, the coating will protect the iron If the coating is damaged or scratched, the iron is still protected from rusting. This is because the zinc is more reactive than the iron and so it will react and corrode instead of the iron.

Zinc blocks are attached to the hulls of ships and will corrode rather than the hull. The zinc is called a sacrificial anode.

QUESTIONS

Q1 **a** Write the balanced chemical equation for the reaction between copper(II) oxide and hydrogen.
b From the reaction what can be said about the reactivity of hydrogen compared to copper?

Q2 Copper (II) sulphate solutions reacts with zinc as shown below:
$CuSO_4(aq) + Zn(s) \rightarrow ZnSO_4(aq) + Cu(s)$
a What type of chemical reaction is this?
b What can be deduced about the relative reactivity of copper and zinc?

Q3 Describe how you would use metals and their oxides in experiments to establish their order of reactivity.

Q4 Zinc prevents iron ships hulls from rusting (corroding).
a What is the name for this process?
b Why does zinc protect iron from rusting?

More questions
on the CD ROM

PREPARING AND ANALYSING

Safety in the laboratory

Videos & questions
on the CD ROM

It is of the **highest importance** that you **work safely** when performing experiments in a chemistry laboratory. These are precautions you should follow:

- Wear **suitable clothing**, e.g. a laboratory coat or other protective clothing.
- Wear **safety goggles** to protect eyes.
- Wear **gloves** to protect hands.
- Perform experiments in a **fume cupboard**.

To work safely with chemicals, it is important to know what dangers they pose. Containers for chemical substances have **hazard symbols** to show what the dangers are. A substance may have more than one symbol.

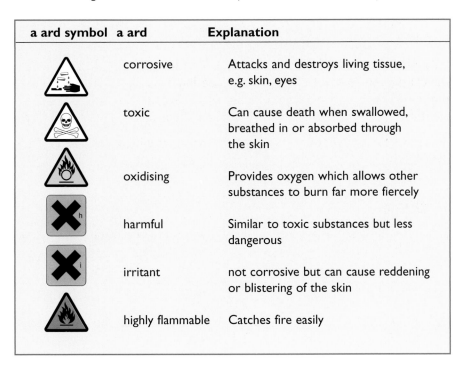

a ard symbol	a ard	Explanation
	corrosive	Attacks and destroys living tissue, e.g. skin, eyes
	toxic	Can cause death when swallowed, breathed in or absorbed through the skin
	oxidising	Provides oxygen which allows other substances to burn far more fiercely
	harmful	Similar to toxic substances but less dangerous
	irritant	not corrosive but can cause reddening or blistering of the skin
	highly flammable	Catches fire easily

Identifying metal ions (cations)

Ions of metals are **cations – positive ions –** and are found in ionic compounds. There are two ways of identifying metal cations:

- *either* from **solids** of the compound
- *or* from **solutions** of the compound.

Metal ions in solids

A. FLAME TESTS

In a flame test, a piece of nichrome wire is dipped into concentrated hydrochloric acid, then into the solid compound, and then into a **blue Bunsen flame**. A colour is seen in the flame which identifies the metal ion in the compound.

The colour of the flame can be used to identify the metal ions present.

Name of ion	Formula of ion	Colour seen in flame
lithium	Li^+	bright red
sodium	Na^+	golden yellow/orange
potassium	K^+	lilac (purple)
calcium	Ca^{2+}	brick red
barium	Ba^+	apple green

A* EXTRA

- All the reactions with sodium hydroxide solution produce insoluble metal hydroxides: $Ca(OH)_2(s)$, $Cu(OH)_2(s)$, $Fe(OH)_2(s)$, $Fe(OH)_3(s)$, $Mg(OH)_2(s)$
- You need to be able to write the formula for these and their ions. Remember: copper and iron are transition metals so the roman numeral tells you the charge on the ion.
- The green $Fe(OH)_2$ oxidises in air ($Fe^{2+} \rightarrow Fe^{3+}$) to form the reddish brown $Fe(OH)_3$.

B. TESTS ON SOLUTIONS IN WATER

Metal ions are found in **ionic compounds**, so most will dissolve in water to form solutions. These **solutions** can be tested with other substances to identify the aqueous cation:

Name of ion in solution	Formula	Test	Result
calcium	$Ca^{2+}(aq)$	Add sodium hydroxide solution in drops. Keep adding until in excess	White precipitate formed which remains even when excess sodium hydroxide solution added
copper(II)	$Cu^{2+}(aq)$	Add sodium hydroxide solution in drops	Light blue precipitate formed
iron(II)	$Fe^{2+}(aq)$	Add sodium hydroxide solution in drops	Green precipitate formed. On standing, changes to reddish brown colour
iron(III)	$Fe^{3+}(aq)$	Add sodium hydroxide solution in drops	Reddish brown precipitate formed
magnesium	$Mg^{2+}(aq)$	Add sodium hydroxide solution in drops. Keep adding until in excess	White precipitate formed which remains, even when excess sodium hydroxide solution is added

Identifying ammonium ions, NH_4^+

The **test** for the **ammonium ion** is as in the diagram.

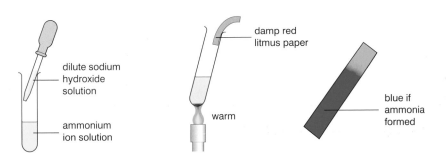

Test for the ammonium ion, NH_4^+.

Identifying anions

As with metal cations, negative ions (anions) are tested as **solids** or as **solutions**.

A. TESTING FOR ANIONS IN SOLIDS
The following test for anions in solids applies only to **carbonates**.

Dilute hydrochloric or sulphuric acid is added to the solid, and any gas produced is passed through limewater. If the limewater goes cloudy/milky, the solid contains a carbonate.

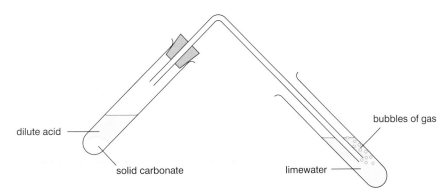

This reaction has been met before:

acid	+	carbonate	→	a salt	+	water	+	carbon dioxide

e.g $2\ HCl$ + Na_2CO_3 → $2\ NaCl$ + H_2O + CO_2

hydrochloric + sodium   sodium + water + carbon dioxide
     acid   carbonate   chloride

e.g. $2\ HNO_3$ + $ZnCO_3$ → $Zn(NO_3)_2$ + $H2O$ + CO_2

nitric acid +   zinc   zinc + water + carbon dioxide
              carbonate   nitrate

Some carbonates undergo thermal decomposition and produce carbon dioxide.

Copper(II) carbonate is a **green** solid which when heated goes **black** and gives off carbon dioxide:

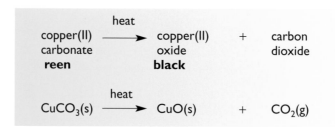

However since not all carbonates do decompose to give carbon dioxide when heated using a dilute acid is the best way of testing for carbonates.

B. TESTING FOR ANIONS IN SOLUTION

Many ionic compounds are soluble in water, and so they form solutions that contain anions.

ame of ion	Formula	Test	Result
chloride	$Cl^-(aq)$	To a solution of the halide ions add: 1. dilute nitric acid 2. silver nitrate solution	white precipitate (of AgCl)
bromide	$Br^-(aq)$		cream precipitate (of AgBr)
iodide	$I^-(aq)$		yellow precipitate (of AgI)
sulphate	$SO_4^{2-}(aq)$	Add: 1. dilute hydrochloric acid 2. barium chloride solution	white precipitate (of $BaSO_4$)
nitrate	$NO_3^-(aq)$	1. Add sodium hydroxide solution and warm 2. Add aluminium powder 3. Test any gas produced with damp red litmus paper	red litmus paper goes blue (ammonia gas is produced)

Test for the halide ions. Left: chloride, white precipitate. Centre: bromide, pale cream precipitate. Right: iodide, pale yellow precipitate.

If the silver halides – AgCl, AgBr and AgI – formed as in the table above, are left to stand in daylight for a while, they go dark grey or black. This is because the light reduces them to silver. This darkening in light is the basis of photographic processes which use silver salts on camera film.

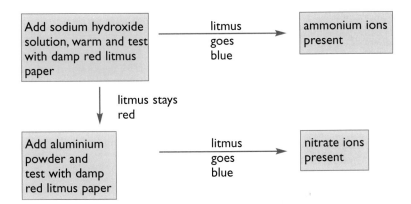

Identifying gases

Many chemical reactions produce a **gas** as one of the products. Identifying the gas is often a step in identifying the **compound** that produced it in the reaction (see 'Testing for anions' on pages 81 and 82).

Gas	Formula	Test	Result of test
hydrogen	H_2	Put in a lighted splint (a flame)	'Pop' or 'squeaky pop' heard (flame usually goes out)
oxygen	O_2	Put in a glowing splint	Splint relights, producing a flame
carbon dioxide	CO_2	Pass gas through limewater	Limewater goes cloudy/milky
chlorine	Cl_2	Put in a piece of damp blue litmus paper	Paper goes red then white (decolourised)
ammonia	NH_3	Put in a piece of damp red litmus or Universal Indicator paper	Paper goes blue
sulphur dioxide	SO_2	Put in a piece of damp potassium dichromate (VI) paper	Colour changes from orange to green

The solubility of salts in water

Here are the general rules that describe the solubility of common types of salts in water
- all common sodium, potassium and ammonium salts are soluble
- all nitrates are soluble
- common chlorides are soluble, except silver chloride.
- common sulphates ae soluble, except barium and calcium
- common carbonates and hydroxides are insoluble, except those of sodium, potassium and ammonium

Making insoluble salts

If two solutions of **soluble salts** are mixed together forming two new salts and one of the products is **insoluble**, the **insoluble salt** forms a **precipitate** – a 'solid made in solution'; see an example on page 20.
The general equation is:

$$\begin{array}{ccccccc} \text{soluble} & + & \text{soluble} & \rightarrow & \text{insoluble} & + & \text{soluble} \\ \text{salt} & & \text{salt} & & \text{salt} & & \text{salt} \\ & & & & \text{(precipitate)} & & \end{array}$$

For example:

$$Na_2CO_3(aq) + CuSO_4(aq) \rightarrow CuCO_3(s) + Na_2SO_4(aq)$$

The **state symbols** show the salts in solution as (aq) and the precipitate – the insoluble salt – as (s).

The practical method involves making a precipitate of an insoluble salt by mixing solutions of two soluble salts.

The flow diagram shows how to make an insoluble salt.

Making insoluble salts.

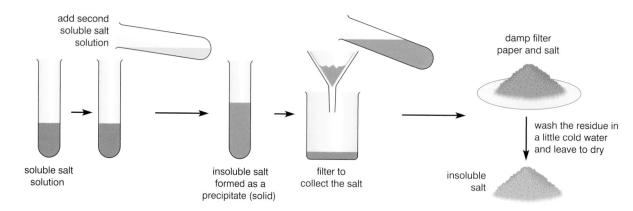

add second soluble salt solution

damp filter paper and salt

soluble salt solution

insoluble salt formed as a precipitate (solid)

filter to collect the salt

insoluble salt

wash the residue in a little cold water and leave to dry

insoluble salt

QUESTIONS

Q1 The jar containing a chemical substance has two hazard labels on it showing it is both corrosive and highly flammable. What safety precautions should be taken when using this substance?

Q2 Describe the test for chlorine gas.

Q3 A white powder is labelled as 'Potassium carbonate'. What two tests could be performed to show it is potassium carbonate?

Q4 How are the following tested to show their presence in a solid?
a The sulphate ion, SO_4^{2-}
b the iodide ion, I^-

More questions on the CD ROM

Living in the age of oil

Ancient alchemists tried to turn cheap metals into gold. They did not succeed, but they gave us the science of chemistry. Today, we extract 'liquid gold' – petroleum – from rocks deep inside the earth, either on land, as in the oil fields of Kuwait and Saudi Arabia, or under the sea, as in the Arabian Gulf and South East Asia. We then turn it into fuel for transport, oil for heating and bitumen for our roads. Petrochemicals made from petroleum are everywhere. Our world depends on synthetic fertilizers, pesticides, drugs, textiles and plastics, and all of these products are based on carbon. Organic chemistry is the study of carbon compounds, and is essential to our modern age.

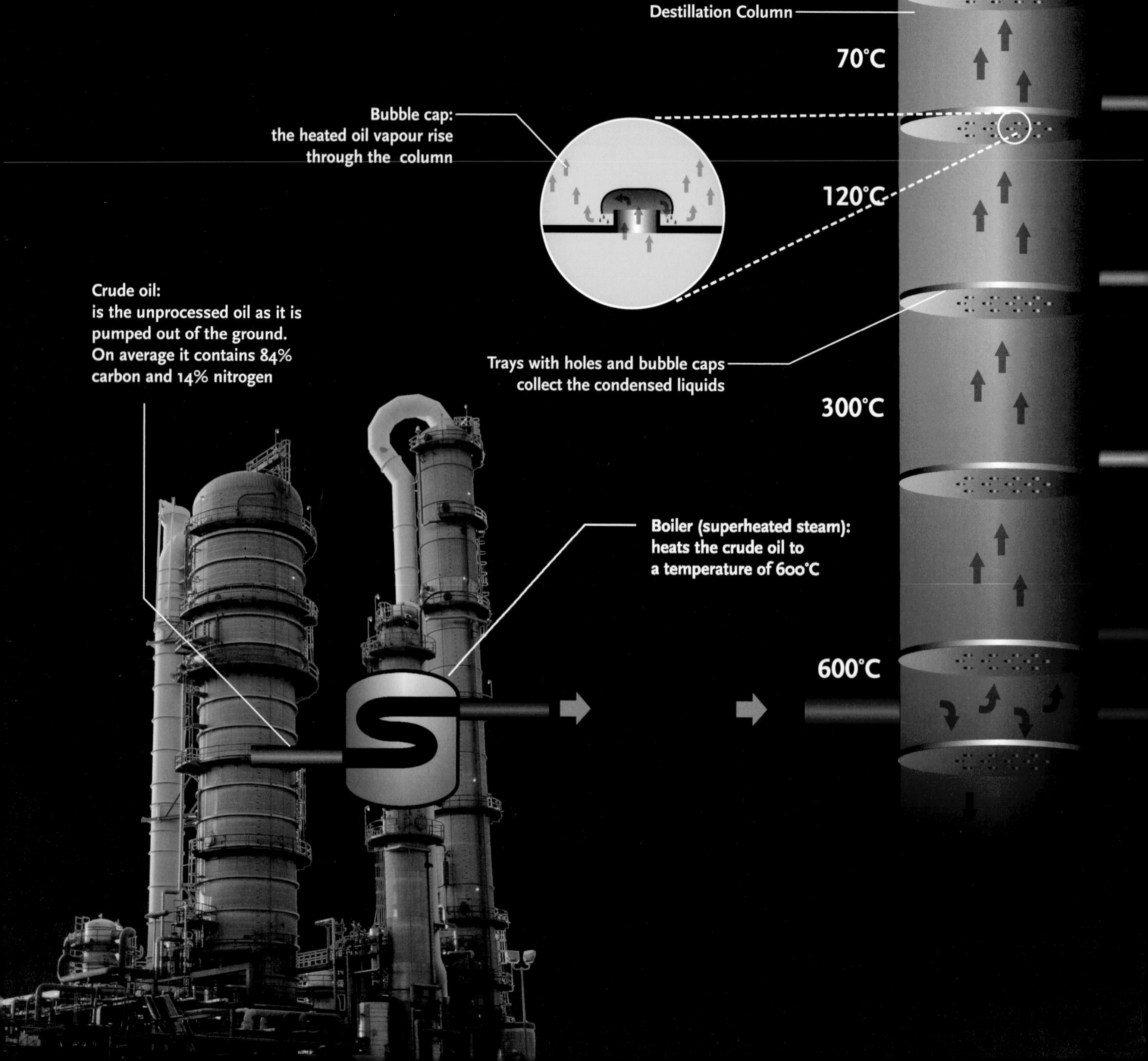

20°C

40°C

Destillation Column

70°C

Bubble cap:
the heated oil vapour rise
through the column

120°C

Crude oil:
is the unprocessed oil as it is
pumped out of the ground.
On average it contains 84%
carbon and 14% nitrogen

Trays with holes and bubble caps
collect the condensed liquids

300°C

Boiler (superheated steam):
heats the crude oil to
a temperature of 600°C

600°C

Chapter 3

ORGANIC CHEMISTRY

Petrolum gas: used for heating, cooking and making plastics

Small alkanes, 1 to 4 carbons

Naphtha: intermediate used in processes making petrol

Alkanes, 5 to 9 carbons

Gasoline: motor fuel

Kerosene: jet-engine fuel, tractor fuel and used making other materials

Alkanes, 5 to 12 carbons

Diesel: fuel and heating oil, used making other materials

Alkanes, 10 to 18 carbons

Lubricating oil: motor oil, grease and other lubricants

Heavy gas, fuel oil: industrial fuel

Residuals: coke, asphalt, tar

Alkanes of 12 and more carbon atoms

Alkanes of 20 to 50 carbon atoms

Alkanes of 50 to 70 carbon atoms

Alkanes of 70 and more carbon atoms

ALKANES

There are two common families of hydrocarbons, the **alkanes** and the **alkenes**. Members of a family have similar chemical properties, and physical properties that change gradually from one member to the next.

Many alkanes are obtained from **crude oil** by **fractional distillation**. The first members of the family are used extensively as fuels. Apart from burning, however, they are remarkably unreactive. Alkanes are made up of atoms joined by single covalent bonds, so they are known as **saturated** hydrocarbons.

		Molecular formula	Displayed formula	Boiling point (°C)	State at room temperature and pressure
Alkanes	methane	CH_4		−162	gas
	ethane	C_2H_6		−89	gas
	propane	C_3H_8		−42	gas
	butane	C_4H_{10}		0	gas
	pentane	C_5H_{12}		36	liquid

Homologous series and general formula

A family of hydrocarbons, such as the alkanes are called a **homologous series**. Each member of a homologous series contains the same functional group.

Each member of a homologous series differs from the one before by one carbon atom. For example, in alkanes the group $-CH_2-$ is added to the chain.

Properties of alkanes

	Alkanes
General formula	$C_nH_{2n} + 2$
Description	saturated (no double C=C bond)
Combustion	burn in oxygen to form CO_2 and H_2O (CO if low supply of oxygen)
Reactivity	low
Chemical test	none
Uses	fuels

Methane is burning in the oxygen in the air to form carbon dioxide and water.

The shape of alkane molecules

In alkanes, the four bonds on each carbon atom are directed to the corners of a tetrahedron.

The **methane** molecule is tetrahedral in shape.

What is isomerism?

The names of hydrocarbons are based on the number of carbon atoms in their molecules. This is the structure of butane (C_4H_{10}):

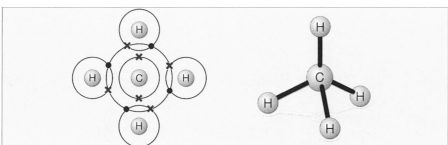

The carbon atoms in a hydrocarbon molecule can be arranged in different ways. For example, in butane, C_4H_{10}, the carbon atoms can be positioned in two ways, while retaining the same molecular formula:

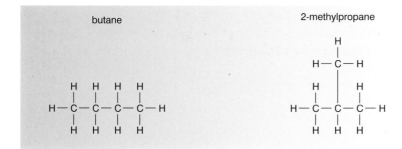

butane   2-methylpropane

2-Methylpropane is a **structural isomer** (same atoms but rearranged) of butane which has a longer chain of carbons. This feature of alkane structure is called **structural isomerism**.

The table shows isomers of the alkane C_5H_{12}.

Isomer	Pentane	2-Methylbutane	2,2-Dimethylpropane
Structure			
Boiling point (°C)	36	27	11

The chlorination of methane

Halogenation is the replacement of one or more hydrogens in an organic compound by halogen atoms.

When methane is reacted with chlorine the products of the reaction depend on whether there is an excess of methane or an excess of chlorine. If there is an excess of methane it forms chloromethane and hydrogen chloride.

methane + chlorine → chloromethane + hydrogen chloride

$$CH_4(g) \ + \ Cl_2(g) \ \rightarrow \ CH_3Cl(g) \ + \ HCl(g)$$

If there is an excess of chlorine then a mixture of products is formed. Chlorine replaces up to 4 of the hdrogen atoms in methane.

QUESTIONS

Q1 What is meant by each of the following?
 a homologous series
 b structural isomerism.

Q2 Give two isomers of butane, C_4H_{10}.

More questions
on the CD ROM

ALKENES

Properties of alkenes

Alkenes are another homologous series, so they have similar chemical properties and physical properties that change gradually from one member to the next.

Alkenes		Molecular formula	Displayed formula	Boiling point (°C)	State at room temperature and pressure
	ethene	C_2H_4		−104	gas
	propene	C_3H_6		−48	gas
	butene	C_4H_8		−6	gas
	pentene	C_5H_{10}		30	liquid

The alkenes are often formed in the cracking process. They contain one or more carbon-carbon double bonds. Hydrocarbons with at least one double bond are known as **unsaturated** hydrocarbons. Alkenes burn well and are reactive in other ways also. Their reactivity is due to the carbon–carbon double bond.

Alkenes can be distinguished from alkanes by adding **bromine water** to the hydrocarbon. Alkanes do not react with bromine water, but an alkene will decolourise it. The type of reaction is known as an **addition** reaction:

| ethene | + | bromine | → | 1,2-dibromoethane |
| (colourless gas) | | (brown liquid) | | (colourless liquid) |

	Alkenes
General formula	C_nH_{2n}
Description	unsaturated (contains a double C=C bond)
Combustion	burn in oxygen to form CO_2 and H_2O (CO if low supply of oxygen)
Reactivity	high (because of double C=C bond) undergo addition reactions
Chemical test	turn bromine water from brown to colourless (an addition reaction)
Uses	making polymers (addition reactions) e.g. polyethene

In alkenes the bonds on each carbon atom are directed to the corners of an equilateral triangle.

Alkenes show the same property, depending on the position of the double C=C bond. For example, alternatives of butene (C_4H_8) structure are:

but-1-ene   but-2-ene

Each carbon atom has four bonds linked to either H atoms or other C atoms by single or double bonds.

Addition reactions of alkenes

Another addition reaction of alkenes is adding hydrogen (in the presence of a catalyst) to make an alkane:

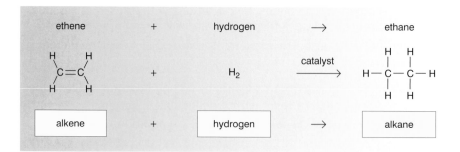

ethene	+	hydrogen	→	ethane
alkene	+	hydrogen	→	alkane

This reaction is used to make **margarine**. Vegetable oils contain unsaturated fats (i.e. fats with C=C double bonds). When hydrogen is added to these fats they become saturated and **harder**, so producing margarine.

Margarine is made of olive oil whose unsaturated molecules have been saturated with hydrogen.

In the bromine water reaction, a bromine water molecule (Br$_2$) splits and the two bromine atoms add on to the atoms either side of the double bond in the alkene.

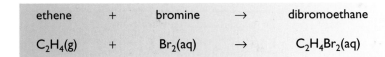

ethene	+	bromine	→	dibromoethane
C$_2$H$_4$(g)	+	Br$_2$(aq)	→	C$_2$H$_4$Br$_2$(aq)

The bromine water becomes colourless because it is the Br$_2$ molecules that give the liquid its brown colour. This can be used as a test for alkenes.

QUESTIONS

Q1 a Draw displayed formulae for hexene.
  b Describe a test that could be used to distinguish between hexane and hexene.

Q2 Draw two isomers of butene.

More questions on the CD ROM

ETHANOL

You should check with your tutor about the aspects of this topic that you will be covering in your studies, before studying this section.

What are alcohols?

Alcohols are molecules containing the **-OH functional group** which is responsible for their properties and reactions.

Alcohols have the general formula $C_nH_{2n+1}OH$ and belong to the same homologous series, part of which is shown below.

Alcohol	Formula	Structure	Boiling point/°C
Methanol	CH_3OH	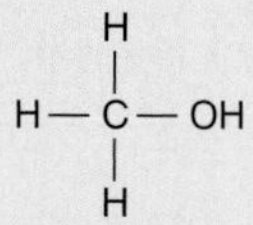	65
Ethanol	C_2H_5OH	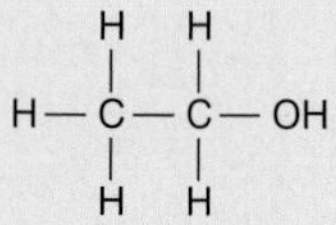	76
Propanol	C_3H_7OH	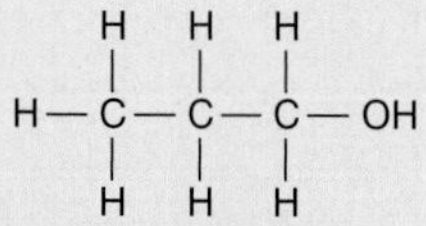	97

Alcohols form structural isomers depending on where the -OH group is placed on the carbon chain. For example:

propan-1-ol

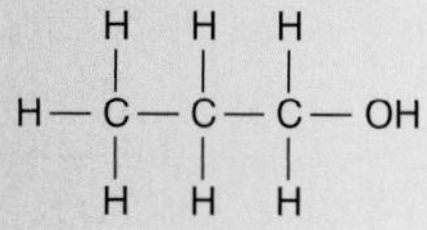

propan-2-ol

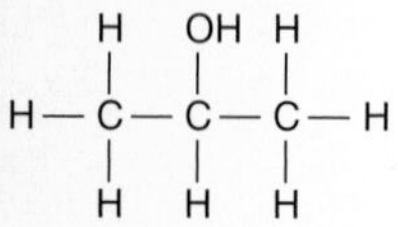

94

Ethanol – the commonest alcohol

Ethanol, commonly just called 'alcohol', is the most widely used of the alcohol family. The major uses of ethanol are given below:

Use of ethanol	Reason
Alcoholic drinks, e.g. wine, beer, spirits	Affects the brain. It is a depressant, so slows reactions. Poisonous in large quantities.
Solvent, e.g. perfumes	The –OH group allows it to dissolve in water, and it dissolves other organic compounds
Fuel, e.g. for cars	It only releases CO_2 and H_2O into the environment, not other pollutant gases as from petrol. It is a renewable resource because it comes from plants, e.g. sugar beet, sugar cane.

Brazilians use Alcool as vehicle fuel. It is made from the fermented and distilled juice of sugar cane.

Ethanol is made by the process of **fermentation**.

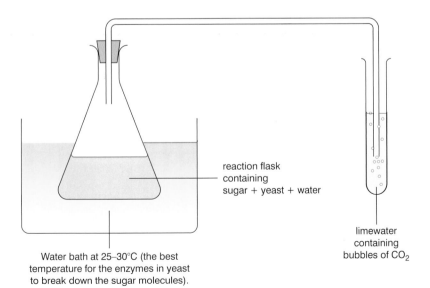

Fermentation apparatus.

reaction flask
containing
sugar + yeast + water

Water bath at 25–30°C (the best temperature for the enzymes in yeast to break down the sugar molecules).

limewater
containing
bubbles of CO_2

95

The chemical reaction for fermentation is:

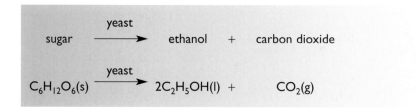

sugar $\xrightarrow{\text{yeast}}$ ethanol + carbon dioxide

$C_6H_{12}O_6(s) \xrightarrow{\text{yeast}} 2C_2H_5OH(l) + CO_2(g)$

The **source** of the sugar determines the type of alcoholic drink produced, for example, grapes for wine, barley for beer.

At the end of the fermentation process, which takes time because it is an enzymic reaction (yeast) and a batch process pure alcohol is extracted by **fractional distillation**. The mixture is boiled and the alcohol vapour reaches the top of the fractionating column where it condenses back to a liquid.

Apparatus for fractional distillation of alcohol.

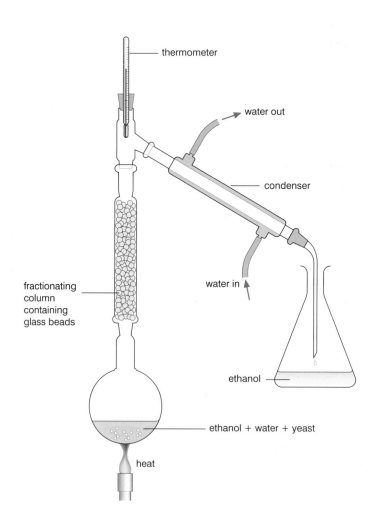

On an **industrial scale**, ethanol is made from alkenes produced by the refining of crude oil. The reaction is:

$$\text{ethene} + \text{steam} \xrightarrow[\substack{\text{phosphoric acid} \\ \text{as catalyst}}]{300°C, 70\ atm} \text{ethanol}$$

These are quite extreme conditions in terms of energy (300 °C) and specialist plant equipment (to generate 70 atmospheres), and so the cost is high.

This process has the advantages over fermentation of being a continuous process and of producing ethanol at a fast rate.

The choice of method in the manufacture of ethanol

The best method for making ethanol depends on local circumstances, for example the relative availability of sugar cane and crude oil.

	Advantage	**Disadvantage**
Fermentation	Uses renewable resources. Flavour of ethanol for alcoholic drinks.	Slow 'batch' process. Only small amount of ethanol produced.
Ethene + steam	Fast 'continuous processes'. Large amounts of ethanol produced.	Uses non-renewable resource. Flavours have to be added artificially for drinks.

The reactions of ethanol (and other alcohols)

The reason why ethanol is such an important chemical compound (as are other alcohols) is that it can be converted into other important compounds.

Ethanol reacts in the following ways because of the –OH functional group:

1 With sodium to give hydrogen gas:

$$\text{sodium} + \text{ethanol} \rightarrow \text{sodium ethanoate} + \text{hydrogen}$$
$$2Na(s) + 2C_2H_5OH(l) \rightarrow 2C_2H_5ONa(s) + H_2(g)$$

2 Ethanol can be oxidised to make ethanoic acid (a carboxylic acid) using an oxidising agent, e.g. potassium dichromate(VI) solution in sulphuric acid.

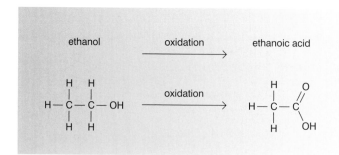

Ethanoic acid is the acid in vinegar. If wine or beer are not properly sealed, the ethanol is oxidised over time by the oxygen in the air and the wine or beer becomes acidic, so spoiling their taste.

Ethanol can be dehydrated to make ethene

Ethanol can be dehydrated to give ethene by heating it with an excess of concentrated sulphuric acid at about 170°C. Concentrated phosphoric(V) acid H_3PO_4 can be used instead.

The acids are used as a **catalyst** so they are not written into the equation:

ethanol   →   ethene   +   water
CH_3CH_2OH → $CH_2 = CH_2$ + H_2O

What are carboxylic acids?

Carboxylic acids make up a homologous series of compounds containing the functional group –COOH.

Acid	Formula	Structure
methanoic acid	HCOOH	H—C with O double bond and OH
ethanoic acid	CH_3COOH	H—C—C with O double bond and OH
propanoic acid	C_2H_5COOH	H—C—C—C with O double bond and OH

The reaction of ethanol with carboxylic acids

Esters are made by reaction with alcohols (with concentrated sulphuric acid as a catalyst):

propanoic acid   +   ethanol   ⇌   ethyl propanoate

The reaction of alcohols with carboxylic acids is called **esterification**. Concentrated sulphuric acid is the catalyst. It works by absorbing the water formed in the reaction. Concentrated sulphuric acid is a **dehydrating agent**.

Esters often have distinct, pleasant smells. They are often used as flavourings or perfumes. For example, methyl butanoate gives pineapple flavour.

QUESTIONS

Q1 In the laboratory fermentation experiment to make ethanol from sugar using yeast, why is it important that
 a the reaction is kept at 25–30°C and not higher than that temperature range?
 b oxygen from the air cannot enter the reaction flask?

Q2 Give the structural formula of two isomers of butanol, C_4H_7OH.

Q3 What is 'esterification'?

More questions on the CD ROM

big

small

PARTICLE SIZE
– the reactants can collide more often

TEMPERATURE
– the particles move more quickly and collide more often

low

high

CONCENTRATION
– more particles means more chances of collisions

low

high

Speeding up and slowing down

In villages all over Asia, people do their daily cooking over fires, which provide heat. In cooking we're using fire to control a chemical process. Without the chemical processes of cooking, we couldn't eat most meat, or plants like rice; or like cassava, which is poisonous if it's not cooked. But if you don't stop the process at the right time, the food becomes inedible again – the process of cooking is all about the rates of reaction. In addition to temperature, rates of reaction are affected by particle size, concentration, the

Chapter 4
PHYSICAL CHEMISTRY

WHAT ARE THE STATES OF MATTER?

Videos & questions on the CD ROM

All matter is made of atoms and they are arranged differently in the three states of matter – **solids**, **liquids** and **gases**. The way the atoms (or particles) are arranged explains the **properties** of the three states. You might also like to go back and look at page 8.

In **solids**, the particles are held tightly together in a **fixed position**, so solids have a **definite shape**. However, the particles are **vibrating** about their fixed positions because they have energy.

In **liquids**, the particles are held tightly together and have enough energy to **move around**. Liquids have **no definite shape** and will take on the shape of the container they are in.

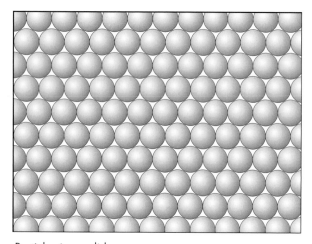
Particles in a solid.

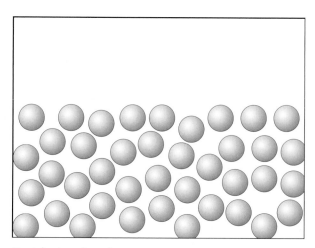
Particles in a liquid.

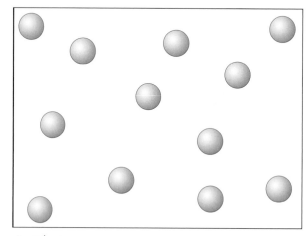
Particles in a gas.

In **gases**, the particles are further apart and have enough energy to **move apart** from each other. Gases can **expand** to fill the container they are in.

Gases can be **compressed** to form liquids by using high pressure and cooling.

How do substances change from one state to another?

To change solids → liquids → gases, **heat** must be put in. The heat provides the particles with enough energy to overcome the forces holding them together. The particles move **further apart** as they change from one state to another. You might also like to go back and look at the illustration on page 11.

These are **endothermic** processes, meaning that energy is absorbed.

To change gases → liquids → solids involves **cooling**, so removing energy. This makes the particles come **closer together** as they change from one state to another.

These are **exothermic** processes, meaning that energy is being given out.

The **temperatures** at which one state changes to another have specific names:

Name of temperature	Change of state
melting point	solid → liquid
boiling point	liquid → gas
freezing point	liquid → solid
condensation point	gas → liquid

The particles in a **liquid** can move around. They have different energies, so some are moving faster than others. The faster particles have enough energy to escape from the surface of the liquid and change into gas molecules – also called vapour molecules. This process is **evaporation**. The rate of evaporation increases with **temperature** since heating gives more particles the energy to be able to escape from the surface.

The diagram summarises the changes in states of matter:

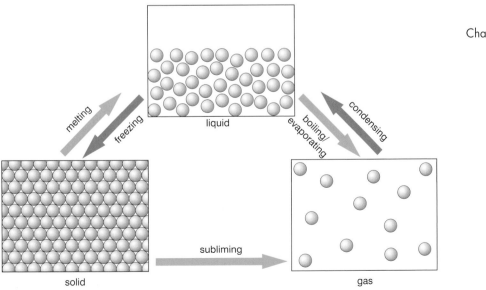

Changes of state.

Mixtures and compounds

A mixture contains two or more substances. No chemical reaction takes place when the mixture is formed. The individual substances in a mixture can be separated quite easily using physical means.

Chemical compounds are formed when atoms join together in a chemical reaction. The properties of a compound are very different from the properties of the components that were used to form the compound. The components can only be separated by a chemical reaction.

How can mixtures be separated?

DISTILLATION

Distilling is a way of separating a mixture of two or more liquids. It relies on the fact that the liquids will boil at different temperatures. For example pure water can be obtained from salt water by distillation.

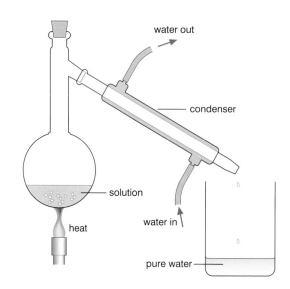

Methods of distillation

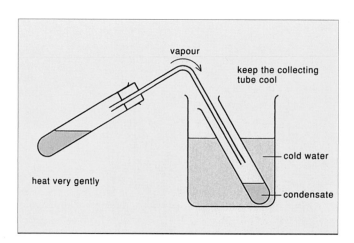

Fractional distillation

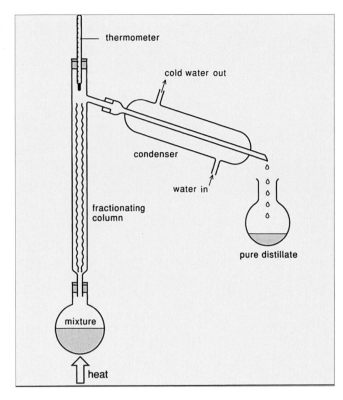

thermometer
cold water out
condenser
water in
fractionating column
pure distillate
mixture
heat

FRACTIONAL DISTILLATION
A fractionating column separates mixture of liquids into different fractions or separate substances.

Fractional distillation is used for oil refining.

FILTRATION
Filtration separates a solid from a liquid. For example, coffee grounds can be separated from the coffee by filtering through a filter paper. The filter paper is like a sieve, it has tiny holes that allow the coffee to pass through but leave the ground coffee behind.

CRYSTALLISATION
If a solid is dissolved in water it can be recovered by evaporation or crystallisation.

When a solution contains as much solute as it can hold at a certain temperature it becomes a **saturated solution**. When a solution is saturated the solute will begin the **crystallise** and it will appear in the solution.

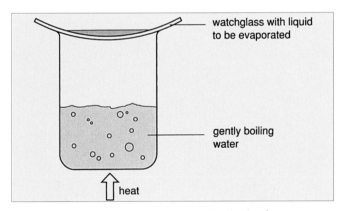

watchglass with liquid to be evaporated

gently boiling water

heat

Methods of evaporation

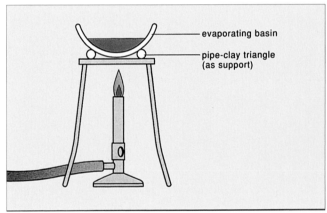

evaporating basin

pipe-clay triangle (as support)

PAPER CHROMATOGRAPHY
Chromatography can be used to separate a mixture of several solids that are soluble. It is often used to separate coloured substances such as inks or dyes (*chroma* means colour).

To separate the different coloured dyes in ink a spot of ink can be dropped into the middle of a filter paper. Water, or another solvent can then be slowly dropped onto the spot.

As the solvent spreads through the paper the dyes are carried in the solvent and then they begin to separate. This happens because the different dyes have different solubilities and so they are carried at different speeds along the paper.

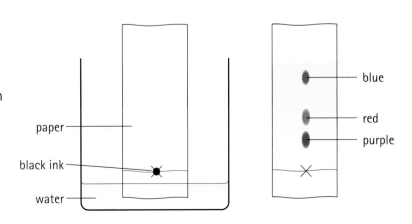

paper
black ink
water

blue
red
purple

What can heating curves show?

When there is a change of state, the **temperature stays the same** as the energy is either being used to separate the particles (heating) or being released as the particles come closer together (cooling).

Heating curve: changes of state when heating a solid.

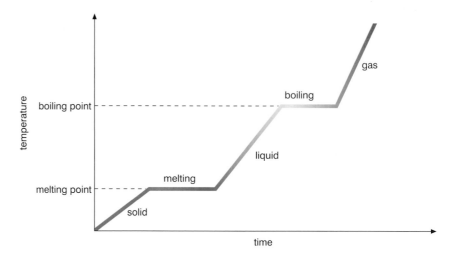

When a liquid turns into a gas (vapour) energy is required to separate the liquid particles and break down the forces between the water molecules. This is called the **the heat of vaporisation**. Heats of vaporisation can be used to compare the energy needed to separate the same number of different particles.

QUESTIONS

Q1 In which state of matter do particles have the most energy? Explain your answer.

Q2 Sodium (melting point 98°C) and aluminium (melting point 660°C) are both metals and are solids at room temperature. From their different melting points, what can you deduce about the forces in the metals?

Q3 Steam at 100°C causes worse burns than water at 100°C. What is the reason for this?

Q4 Why does ice that is melting remain at 0°C until it has all changed to water?

Q5 What change of state is taking place according to the following equation? Hg(g) → Hg(l)

More questions on the CD ROM

ACIDITY, ALKALINITY AND NEUTRALISATION

Aqueous solutions

Videos & questions on the CD ROM

When any substance dissolves in water, it forms an **aqueous solution** shown by the state symbol (aq). Aqueous solutions can be acidic, alkaline or neutral.

Indicators are used to tell if a solution is acidic, alkaline or neutral. Indicators can be used either as liquids or in paper form, and they become different colours with **different solutions**.

The commonest indicator is **litmus** and its colours are shown in the table below:

Colour of litmus	Type of solution
red	acidic
purple	neutral
blue	alkaline

Universal Indicator can show the **strengths** of the acids and alkalis because it has more colours. Each colour is linked to a number called the **pH scale**. The range of numbers is from 1 to 14.

The pH scale.

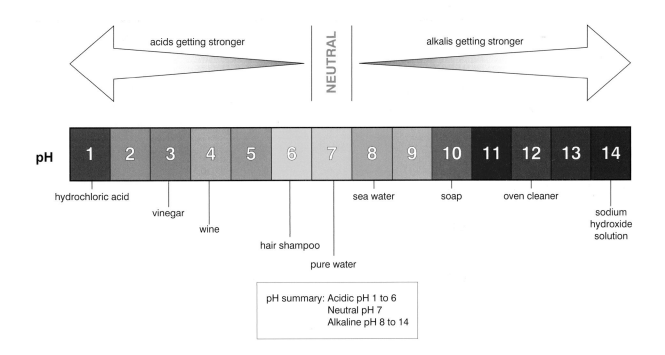

pH summary: Acidic pH 1 to 6
Neutral pH 7
Alkaline pH 8 to 14

Phenolphthalein indicator is colourless in acid solution but turns pink in alkaline solution.

Methyl orange indicator is pink in acid solution and yellow in alkaline solution.

What are acids?

Acids are substances that contain **replaceable hydrogen atoms**. These hydrogen atoms are replaced in chemical reactions by metal atoms, and the compound formed is a **salt**.

Acids only show their acidic properties when **water** is present. This is because, in water, acids form hydrogen ions, H^+ (which are also **protons**) and it is these ions that are responsible for acidic properties. For example:

$$HCl(aq) \rightarrow H^+(aq) + Cl^-(aq)$$

Basicity is the term used to describe how many hydrogen ions an acid molecule can have replaced. The table shows the basicity of some common acids.

Acid	Basicity of acid
hydrochloric acid, HCl	monobasic (one H^+)
nitric acid, HNO_3	monobasic (one H^+)
sulphuric acid, H_2SO_4	dibasic (two H^+'s)
phosphoric acid, H_3PO_4	tribasic (three H^+'s)

Types of acids

HCl, HNO_3, H_2SO_4 and H_3PO_4 are called strong acids because in water they fully dissociate (split up) into ions. They produce all the hydrogen ions available in the molecules, and this is shown by the use of the $\rightarrow$ symbol. For example:

$$HNO_3(aq) \rightarrow H^+(aq) + NO_3^-(aq)$$

$$H_2SO_4(aq) \rightarrow 2H^+(aq) + SO_4^{2-}(aq)$$

Acids which only **partially dissociate into ions**, and so do not release all their hydrogen ions, are called **weak acids**. The molecules of these weak acids are in equilibrium with their ions, as shown by the symbol $\rightleftharpoons$ in an equation.

Ethanoic acid, CH_3COOH, which is the acid found in vinegar, is the best-known example of a weak acid:

$$CH_3COOH(aq) \rightleftharpoons CH_3COO^-(aq) + H^+(aq)$$

What are bases and alkalis?

The oxides and hydroxides of metals are called **bases**.

If the oxide or hydroxide of a metal dissolves in water, it is also called an **alkali**. Alkalis have pHs in the range 8–14. For example:

sodium + oxygen	$\rightarrow$	sodium oxide
$4Na(s) + O_2(g)$	$\rightarrow$	$2Na_2O(s)$
sodium oxide + water	$\rightarrow$	sodium hydroxide
$Na_2O(s) + H_2O(l)$	$\rightarrow$	$2NaOH(aq)$

The sodium oxide above is a **base** because it is the oxide of the metal sodium. In addition, it dissolves in water to form the **alkali** sodium hydroxide.

A* EXTRA

- Ethanoic acid has four hydrogen atoms in its molecule, but only one is released in water – it is monobasic. You need to remember this fact so that you can write the correct equation for its partial dissociation.
- Methanoic acid belongs to the same carboxylic acid family as ethanoic acid. It is also monobasic: $HCOOH(aq) \rightleftharpoons HCOO^-(aq) + H^+(aq)$

Arrhenius described alkalis as substances that 'dissolve in water to form hydroxide ions', OH^-. For example:

$$NaOH(aq) \rightarrow Na^+(aq) + OH^-(aq)$$

Another common alkali is potassium hydroxide, KOH.

NaOH and KOH are **strong alkalis** because they **fully dissociate** to release all the hydroxide ions. This is shown in the equation by the use of the $\rightarrow$ symbol, in exactly the same way as for strong acids. An example is:

$$KOH(aq) \rightarrow K^+(aq) + OH^-(aq)$$

An example of a **weak base** (weak alkali) is ammonia solution, $NH_3(aq)$, which is also called ammonium hydroxide solution, $NH_4OH(aq)$:

$$\text{Either: } NH_3(g) + H_2O(l) \rightleftharpoons NH_4^+(aq) + OH^-(aq)$$

$$\text{or: } NH_4OH(aq) \rightleftharpoons NH_4^+(aq) + OH^-(aq)$$

The use of the symbol $\rightleftharpoons$ shows that the reaction is in equilibrium, and so there is only **partial dissociation**.

Making salts

On the previous page, it was explained that acids contain **replaceable hydrogen atoms**, and that when **metal atoms** take their place, a compound called a **salt** is formed. The names of salts have two parts, as shown:

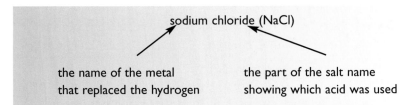

sodium chloride (NaCl)

the name of the metal that replaced the hydrogen

the part of the salt name showing which acid was used

The table shows the four commonest acids and their salt names.

Acid	Salt name
hydrochloric (HCl)	chloride (Cl^-)
nitric (HNO_3)	nitrate (NO_3^-)
sulphuric (H_2SO_4)	sulphate (SO_4^{2-})
phosphoric (H_3PO_4)	phosphate (PO_4^{3-})

Sodium chloride crystals.

Salts are **ionic compounds** where the first part of the name is of the metal ion which is a positive ion (cation), and the second part of the name is from the acid and is a negative ion (anion). For example:

copper(II) sulphate: $\qquad Cu^{2+}$ and $SO_4^{2-} \rightarrow CuSO_4$

Salts are often found in the form of **crystals**. Salt crystals often contain **water of crystallisation** which is responsible for their crystal shapes. Water of crystallisation is shown in the chemical formula of a salt. For example:

| copper(II) sulphate crystals | $CuSO_4.5H_2O$ |
| iron(II) sulphate crystals | $FeSO_4.7H_2O$ |

Copper(II) sulphate crystals.

Making salts

There are five methods for making salts: four make **soluble salts** and one makes **insoluble salts**.

MAKING SOLUBLE SALTS

> 1.   Acid + alkali $\rightarrow$ a salt + water
> e.g. $HCl(aq) + NaOH(aq) \rightarrow NaCl(aq) + H_2O(l)$
>
> 2.   Acid + base $\rightarrow$ a salt + water
> e.g. $H_2SO_4(aq) + CuO(s) \rightarrow CuSO_4(aq) + H_2O(l)$
>
> 3.   Acid + carbonate $\rightarrow$ a salt + water + carbon dioxide
> e.g. $2HNO_3(aq) + CuCO_3(s) \rightarrow Cu(NO_3)_2(aq) + H_2O(l) + CO_2(g)$
>
> 4.   Acid + metal $\rightarrow$ a salt + hydrogen
> e.g. $2HCl(aq) + Mg(s) \rightarrow MgCl_2(aq) + H_2(g)$

The four general equations above are best remembered by the initials of the reactants:

> A (acid) + A (alkali)
> A (acid) + B (base)
> A (acid) + C (carbonate)
> A (acid) + M (metal)

The symbol '(aq)' after the formula of the salt shows that it is a **soluble salt**.

Neutralisation is the specific term used for the reactions of **acids** with **alkalis** and **bases**. When acids react with alkalis, the reaction is between H^+ ions and OH^- ions to make water, as:

> $H^+(aq) + OH^-(aq) \rightarrow H_2O(l)$

Reactions of acids with alkalis are used in the experimental procedure of **titration**, in which solutions react together to give the end-point shown by an indicator. Calculations are then performed to find the concentration of the acid or the alkali.

IN THE LABORATORY

Of the *four* methods for making soluble salts, symbol (aq), only *one* uses solution A(aq) + solution B(aq).

> *Method 1 (neutralisation):*
>
> acid(aq) + alkali(aq) $\rightarrow$ a salt(aq) + water(l)

The other three methods involve adding a solid(s) to a solution(aq).

> *Method 2:*
>
> acid(aq) + base(s) $\rightarrow$ a salt(aq) + water(l)
>
> *Method 3:*
>
> acid(aq) + carbonate(s) $\rightarrow$ a salt(aq) + water(l) + carbon dioxide(g)
>
> *Method 4:*
>
> acid(aq) + metal(s) $\rightarrow$ a salt(aq) + hydrogen(g)

A* EXTRA

- Because acids form H^+ ions and alkalis form OH^- ions in water, the neutralisation reaction of acids with alkalis is an application of Arrhenius's theory: $H^+(aq) + OH^-(aq) \rightarrow H_2O(l)$
  You can make the answer to questions about Arrhenius's theory much more powerful by quoting this example of the 'neutralisation process'.

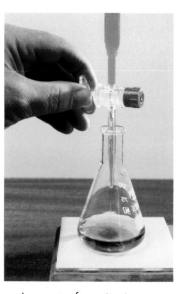

Apparatus for a titration.

The flow diagram shows how to make soluble salts from solids.

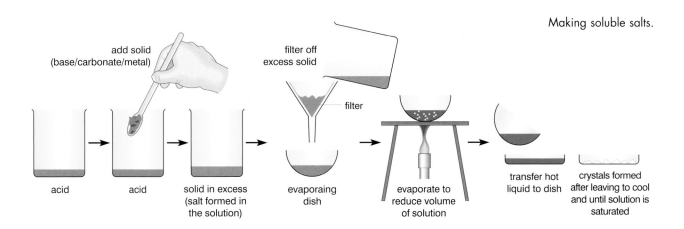

Making soluble salts.

acid · acid · solid in excess (salt formed in the solution) · add solid (base/carbonate/metal) · filter off excess solid · filter · evaporaing dish · evaporate to reduce volume of solution · transfer hot liquid to dish · crystals formed after leaving to cool and until solution is saturated

Acid–alkali titration

Titration is an accurate experimental method of finding the concentration of an acid or an alkali using the neutralisation reaction.

Method:

1. 25.0 cm^3 of the acid/alkali of unknown concentration is put into a conical flask using a pipette. The flask is stood on a white tile (to see colour changes more easily) and a few drops of an appropriate indicator are added.
2. The burette is filled with an alkali/acid of known concentration.
3. By opening the burette tap the alkali/acid is run into the conical flask.
4. Near the 'end-point' (neutralisation point when the indicator will change colour) the solution is added drop-wise until one drop changes the colour of the indicator.
5. The volume of solution added from the burette is read and the whole process repeated until burette readings that are identical (or within 0.10 cm^3 obtained).
6. The burette volume is used to calculate the concentration of the alkali/acid.

A* EXTRA

- The concentration of a solution is often expressed in terms of mol dm^{-3}. A 1 mol dm^{-3} solution contains 1 mole of solute dissolved to make 1 dm^3 (1000 cm^3) of solution.

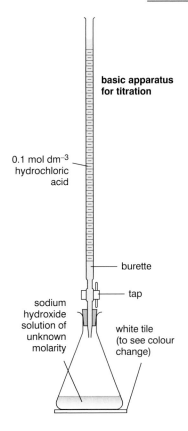

basic apparatus for titration

0.1 mol dm^{-3} hydrochloric acid

burette

tap

sodium hydroxide solution of unknown molarity

white tile (to see colour change)

WORKED EXAMPLE

25.00 cm^3 of sodium hydroxide solution required 30.00 cm^3 of 2.00 mol dm^{-3} hydrochloric acid for neutralisation.

What is the concentration of the sodium hydroxide solution?

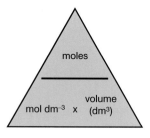

This triangle will help you to calculate concentrations of solutions.

HCl (aq) + NaOH (aq) → NaCl(aq) + H2O (l)

Moles HCl added = $\dfrac{30.00}{1000} \times 2 = 0.060$

From the equation the ratio of HCl : NaOH is 1:1 so

Moles NaOH = 0.060

Concentration of NaOH = $\dfrac{1000 \times 0.060}{25.00} = 2.40$ mol dm^{-3}

QUESTIONS

Q1 **a** What is an indicator?

　　b What is the pH scale?
　　c How are Universal Indicator and the pH scale linked?

Q2 Phosphoric acid, H$_3$PO$_4$, is a strong acid.
　　a What is meant by a 'strong acid'?
　　b Write the balanced chemical equation (including state symbols) for phosphoric acid producing ions when dissolved in water.
　　c What would be the pH of phosphoric acid?

Q3 Methanoic acid, HCOOH, is a weak acid.
　　a What is meant by 'weak acid'?
　　b Write the balanced chemical equation for methanoic acid dissolving in water to produce ions.

Q4 Complete the following equations and include state symbols:

a 2KOH(aq) + H$_2$SO$_4$(aq) → _____ + _____

b 2HCl(aq) + MgO(s) → _____ + _____

c 2HNO$_3$(aq) + BaCO$_3$(s) → _____ + _____ + _____

d 2HCl(aq) + Zn(s) _____ + _____

e ZnCl$_2$(aq) + K$_2$CO$_3$(aq) → _____ + _____

More questions on the CD ROM

ENERGETICS

Energy changes in chemical reactions

In most reactions, energy is transferred to the surroundings and the temperature goes up. These reactions are **exothermic**. In a minority of cases, energy is absorbed from the surroundings as a reaction takes place and the temperature goes down. These reactions are **endothermic**.

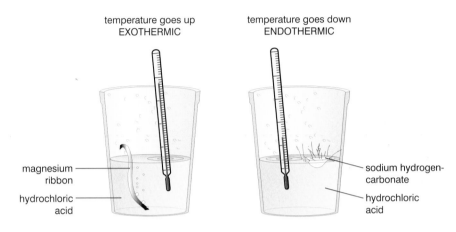

temperature goes up
EXOTHERMIC

temperature goes down
ENDOTHERMIC

magnesium ribbon

hydrochloric acid

sodium hydrogen-carbonate

hydrochloric acid

Energy transfers in a wide range of chemical reactions can be measured using a polystyrene cup as a calorimeter. If a lid is put on the cup, very little energy is transferred to the air and quite accurate results can be obtained.

All reactions involving the combustion of fuels are exothermic. The energy transferred when a fuel burns can be measured using a **calorimetric technique**, as shown in the diagram on the right.

The rise in temperature of the water is a measure of the energy transferred to the water. This technique will not give a very accurate answer because much of the energy will be transferred to the surrounding air. Nevertheless, the technique can be used to compare the energy released by the same amounts of different fuels.

The heat energy in chemical reactions is called enthalpy. The **enthalpy change** is given the symbol ΔH. The enthalpy change for a particular reaction is shown at the end of the balanced equation. The units are (k)J mol^{-1}. Example:

400 g of water

metal can

draught excluder

paraffin burner

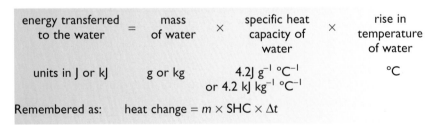

energy transferred to the water	=	mass of water	×	specific heat capacity of water	×	rise in temperature of water
units in J or kJ		g or kg		4.2J g^{-1} °C^{-1} or 4.2 kJ kg^{-1} °C^{-1}		°C
Remembered as:		heat change = $m \times$ SHC $\times \Delta t$				

Measuring the energy produced on burning a liquid fuel.

Units are important in this equation, that is, when you use g for mass of water, then the heat change is in J, but using kg for the mass gives the heat change in kJ.

Since 1 cm^3 of water weighs 1 g, the mass of water in the beaker is the same as the volume of water in cm^3.

The principle of conservation of energy says that energy cannot be created or destroyed. Heat created by a chemical reaction is a form of energy. The rise in temperature of the water shows that energy has been transferred to the water. So it must have come from the chemical reaction occurring.

WORKED EXAMPLE

2.0 g of paraffin were burned in a spirit burner under a metal can containing 400 cm³ of water. The temperature of the water rose from 20 °C to 70 °C. Calculate the energy produced by the paraffin in J g⁻¹ and kJ g⁻¹.

Equation:	heat change	=	mass of water × 4.2 × temperature change
Substitute values:	heat change	=	400 × 4.2 × 50
Calculate:	heat change	=	84000 J per 2 g of paraffin
		=	42000 J g⁻¹
		=	42 kJ g⁻¹

Energy profiles and ΔH

Energy level diagrams show the enthalpy difference between the reactants and products.

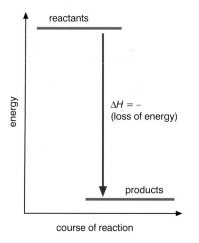

ΔH with a negative value

An **exothermic** reaction. Energy is being lost to the surroundings. ΔH is **negative**.

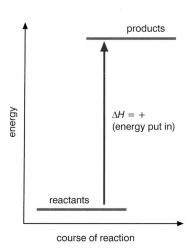

ΔH with a positive value

An **endothermic** reaction. Energy is being absorbed from the surroundings. ΔH is **positive**.

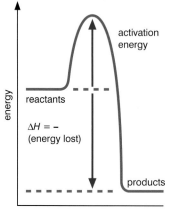

An energy profile for an exothermic reaction.

All ΔH values should have a – or + sign in front of them to show if they are exothermic or endothermic.

Activation energy is the minimum amount of energy required for a reaction to occur. This diagram shows the activation energy of a reaction.

The energy profile can now be completed as shown left. The reaction for this profile is exothermic, with ΔH negative.

Where does the energy come from?

When a fuel is burnt the reaction can be considered to take place in two stages. In the first stage the **covalent bonds** between the atoms in the fuel molecules and the oxygen molecules are **broken**. In the second stage the atoms combine and **new covalent bonds are formed**. For example, in the combustion of propane:

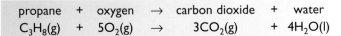

| propane | + | oxygen | $\rightarrow$ | carbon dioxide | + | water |
| $C_3H_8(g)$ | + | $5O_2(g)$ | $\rightarrow$ | $3CO_2(g)$ | + | $4H_2O(l)$ |

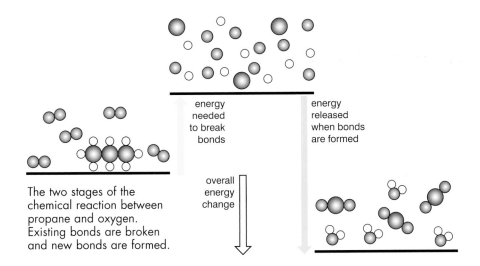

The two stages of the chemical reaction between propane and oxygen. Existing bonds are broken and new bonds are formed.

energy needed to break bonds

energy released when bonds are formed

overall energy change

Stage 1: Energy is needed (absorbed from the surroundings) to break the bonds. This process is endothermic.

Stage 2: Energy is released (transferred to the surroundings) as the bonds form. This process is exothermic.

The overall reaction is exothermic because more energy is released when bonds are formed than is needed initially to break the bonds. A simplified **energy level diagram** showing the exothermic nature of the reaction is shown on the right.

The larger the alkane molecule, the more the energy that is released on combustion. This is because, although more bonds have to be broken in the first stage of the reaction, more bonds are formed in the second stage.

The increase in energy from one alkane to the next is almost constant, due to the extra CH_2 unit in the molecule.

In the table the energy released on combustion has been worked out per mole of alkane. In this way a comparison can be made when the same number of molecules of each alkane is burnt.

Alkane	Energy of combustion (kJ mol⁻¹)
methane CH_4	882
ethane C_2H_6	1542
propane C_3H_8	2202
butane C_4H_{10}	2877
pentane C_5H_{12}	3487
hexane C_6H_{14}	4141

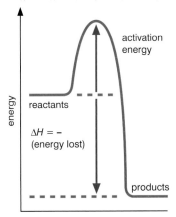

activation energy

energy

reactants

$\Delta H = -$
(energy lost)

products

course of reaction

An energy profile for an exothermic reaction.

A* EXTRA

- In an exothermic reaction the energy released on forming new bonds is greater than that needed to break the old bonds.
- In an endothermic reaction more energy is needed to break bonds than is released when new bonds are formed. The energy changes in endothermic reactions are usually relatively small.

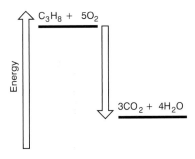

C_3H_8 + $5O_2$

Energy

$3CO_2$ + $4H_2O$

Bond energy calculations

Every covalent bond has a particular amount of energy needed to break it. This is the same as the amount of energy given out when it is made. This is the **bond energy** and its units are kJ mol^{-1}.

The table shows some values of bond energies.

bond	C–C	C–H	O=O	H–H	H–O	C=O	Cl–Cl	H–Cl
bond energy (kJ mol^{-1})	348	413	498	436	464	745	242	431

WORKED EXAMPLE

Calculate the energy change for the reaction between hydrogen and chlorine:

$$H_2 + Cl_2 \rightarrow 2HCl \qquad \text{i.e. } H\text{–}H + Cl\text{–}Cl \rightarrow 2 \times H\text{–}Cl$$

What does the sign of the energy change tell you about the reaction?

H–H	+	Cl–Cl	→	2 × H–Cl
436 kJ mol^{-1}		242 kJ mol^{-1}		2 × 431 kJ mol^{-1}

total for bonds
= + 678 kJ mol^{-1}
(endothermic because bond breaking)

total for bonds
= − 862 kJ mol^{-1}
(exothermic because bond making)

Overall difference − 862 kJ mol^{-1}
+ 678 kJ mol^{-1}
− 184 kJ mol^{-1}

Answer: ΔH = −184 kJ mol^{-1}
It is an exothermic reaction (negative).

Summary of method:
1. Total all the bonds on the left and allocate a + sign.
2. Total all the bonds on the right and allocate a − sign.
3. Find the difference between the two values, not forgetting the sign (+ or −).
4. State if exothermic (−) or endothermic (+).

A* EXTRA

- It is essential in bond energy calculation questions to identify the sign of the value and link it to exothermic (-) or endothermic (+). You will gain extra credit for linking 'exothermic' to more energy being released by bond making than used in bond breaking, and the reverse for 'endothermic'.

QUESTIONS

Q1 A 0.2 g strip of magnesium ribbon is added to 40 cm³ of hydrochloric acid in a polystyrene beaker. The temperature rises by 32°C. (The specific heat capacity of the hydrochloric acid can be assumed to be the same as that of water, i.e. 4.2 J g⁻¹ °C⁻¹.) Calculate
  a the energy released in the reaction
  b the energy released per gram of magnesium.

Q2 Calcium oxide reacts with water as shown in the equation:
$CaO(s) + H_2O(l) \rightarrow Ca(OH)_2(s)$
An energy level diagram for this reaction is shown below.

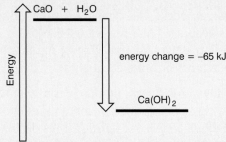

  a What does the energy level diagram tell us about the type of energy change that takes place in this reaction?
  b What does the energy level diagram indicate about the amounts of energy required to break bonds and form new bonds in this reaction?

Q3 Chlorine (Cl_2) and hydrogen (H_2) react together to make hydrogen chloride (HCl). The equation can be written as:
H–H + Cl–Cl → H–Cl + H–Cl
When this reaction occurs, energy is transferred to the surroundings. Explain this in terms of the energy transfer processes taking place when bonds are broken and when bonds are made.

Q4 **a** Calculate the energy change for the combustion of methane (CH_4) in oxygen (O_2).

$$H-\underset{\underset{H}{|}}{\overset{\overset{H}{|}}{C}}-H + 2 \times O{=}O \rightarrow O{=}C{=}O + 2 \times H-O-H$$

Use the bond energy values in the text.

  b What does the sign of the energy change tell you about the reaction?

More questions on the CD ROM

RATES OF REACTION

What happens in chemical reactions?

A chemical change, or **chemical reaction**, is quite different from the physical changes that occur, for example, when sugar dissolves in water.

One or more **new substances** are produced.

In many cases an **observable change** is apparent, for example the colour changes or a gas is produced.

An **apparent change in mass** can occur. This change is often quite small and difficult to detect unless accurate balances are used. Mass is conserved in a chemical reaction – the apparent change in mass usually occurs because one of the reactants or products is a gas.

An **energy change** is almost always involved. In most cases energy is released and the surroundings become warmer. In some cases energy is absorbed from the surroundings and so the surroundings become colder. Note: Some physical changes, such as evaporation, also produce energy changes.

Collision theory

For a chemical reaction to occur, the reacting particles (atoms, molecules or ions) must **collide**. The energy involved in the collision must be enough to break the chemical bonds in the reacting particles – or the particles will just bounce off one another.

A collision that has enough energy to result in a chemical reaction is an **effective collision**.

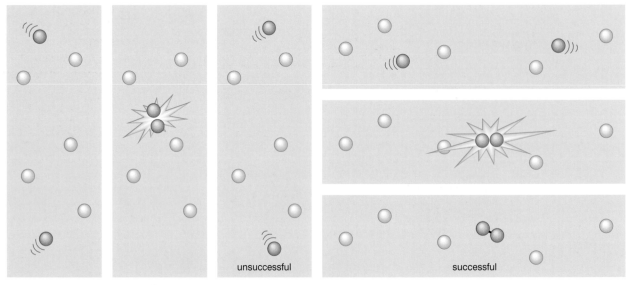

unsuccessful   successful

Particles must collide with sufficient energy to make an effective collision.

Some chemical reactions occur extremely quickly (for example, the explosive reaction between petrol and oxygen in a car engine) and some more slowly (for example, iron rusts over days or weeks). This is because they have different **activation energies**. Activation energy is the minimum amount of energy required in a collision for a reaction to occur. As a general rule, the bigger the activation energy the slower the reaction will be at a particular temperature.

Rate of a reaction

A quick reaction takes place in a short time. It has a high **rate of reaction**. As the time taken for a reaction to be completed increases, the rate of the reaction decreases. In other words:

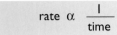

$$\text{rate } \alpha \ \frac{1}{\text{time}}$$

Speed	Rate	Time
quick or fast	high	short
slow	low	long

Monitoring the rate of a reaction

When marble (calcium carbonate) reacts with hydrochloric acid, the following reaction starts straight away:

calcium carbonate	+	hydrochloric acid	→	calcium chloride	+	carbon dioxide	+	water
$CaCO_3(s)$	+	$2HCl(aq)$	→	$CaCl_2(aq)$	+	$CO_2(g)$	+	$H_2O(l)$

The reaction can be monitored as it proceeds either by measuring the **volume of** gas being formed, or by measuring the **change in mass** of the reaction flask.

The volume of gas can be measured every 10 seconds.

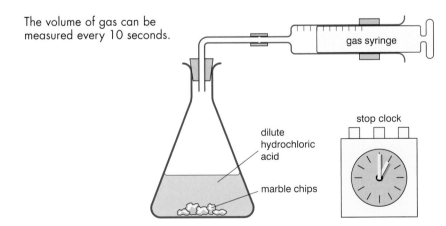

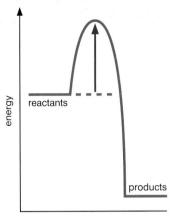

course of reaction

If the activation energy of a reaction is low, more of the collisions will be effective and the reaction will proceed quickly. If the activation energy is high a smaller proportion of collisions will be effective and the reaction will be slow.

A* EXTRA

- The 'barrier' preventing a reaction from occurring is called the activation energy. An effective collision is one which has energy greater than the activation energy and so will lead to a reaction.

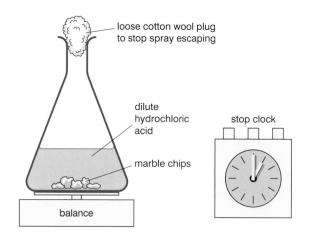

loose cotton wool plug
to stop spray escaping

dilute
hydrochloric
acid

stop clock

marble chips

balance

The change in mass
can be measured
every 10 seconds.
The carbon dioxide
produced in the
reaction escapes into
the air. The cotton
wool plug is there to
stop acid spray from
escaping.

Graphs of the results from both experiments have almost identical shapes.

The rate of the reaction decreases as the reaction proceeds.

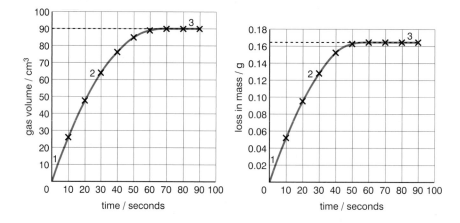

The **rate of the reaction** at any point can be calculated from the **gradient** of the curve. The shapes of the graphs can be divided into three regions:

1 At this point, the curve is the steepest (has the greatest gradient) and the reaction has its highest rate. The maximum number of reacting particles are present and the number of effective collisions per second is at its greatest.

2 The curve is not as steep (has a lower gradient) at this point and the rate of the reaction is lower. Fewer reacting particles are present and so the number of effective collisions per second will be less.

3 The curve is horizontal (gradient is zero) and the reaction is complete. At least one of the reactants has been completely used up and so no further collisions can occur between the two reactants. gas being formed or by measuring the **change in mass** of the reaction flask.

What can change the rate of a reaction?

There are six key factors that can change the rate of a reaction:
- **concentration** (of a solution)
- **temperature**
- **surface area** (of a solid)
- a **catalyst**
- **pressure** (of a gas)
- **light**.

A simple **collision theory** can be used to explain how these factors affect the rate of a reaction. Two important parts of the theory are:

1 The reacting particles must collide with each other.

2 There must be sufficient energy in the collision to overcome the activation energy.

Concentration

Increasing the concentration of a reactant will **increase the rate** of a reaction. When a piece of magnesium ribbon is added to a solution of hydrochloric acid, the following reaction occurs:

magnesium	+	hydrochloric acid	$\rightarrow$	magnesium chloride	+	hydrogen
$Mg(s)$	+	$2HCl(aq)$	$\rightarrow$	$MgCl_2(aq)$	+	$H_2(g)$

As the magnesium and acid come into contact, there is effervescence – 'fizzing', and hydrogen gas is given off. Two experiments were performed using the same length of magnesium ribbon, but different concentrations of acid. In experiment 1 the hydrochloric acid used was 2.0 mol dm^{-3}, in experiment 2 the acid was 0.5 mol dm^{-3}. The graph below shows the results of the two experiments.

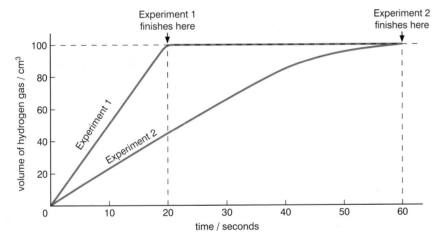

In experiment 1 the curve is steeper (has a greater gradient) than in experiment 2. In experiment 1 the reaction is complete after 20 seconds, whereas in experiment 2 it takes 60 seconds. The rate of the reaction is higher with 2.0 mol dm^{-3} hydrochloric acid than with 0.5 mol dm^{-3} hydrochloric acid. In the 2.0 mol dm^{-3} hydrochloric acid solution the hydrogen ions are more likely to collide with the surface of the magnesium ribbon than in the 0.5 mol dm^{-3} hydrochloric acid.

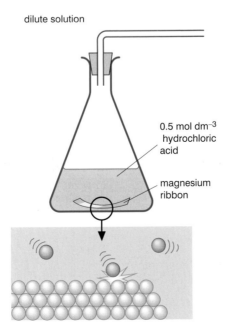

dilute solution

0.5 mol dm^{-3} hydrochloric acid

magnesium ribbon

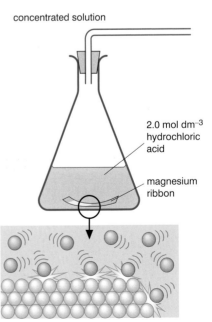

concentrated solution

2.0 mol dm^{-3} hydrochloric acid

magnesium ribbon

Temperature

Increasing the temperature will **increase the rate** of reaction. Warming a chemical transfers kinetic energy to the chemical's particles. More kinetic energy means that the particles move faster. As they are moving faster there will be more collisions each second. The increased energy of the collisions also means that the proportion of collisions that are effective will increase.

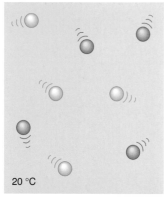

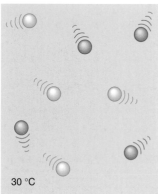

Increasing the temperature of a reaction such as that between calcium carbonate and hydrochloric acid will not increase the final amount of carbon dioxide produced. The **same amount** of gas will be produced in a **shorter time**.

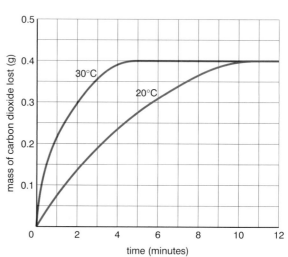

The rates of the two reactions are different but the final loss in mass is the same.

Surface area

Increasing the surface area of a solid reactant will **increase the rate** of a reaction. The reaction can only take place if the reacting particles collide. This means that the reaction takes place at the surface of the solid. The particles within the solid cannot react until those on the surface have reacted and moved away.

Powdered calcium carbonate has a much larger surface area than the same mass of marble chips. A lump of coal will burn slowly in the air whereas coal dust can react explosively.

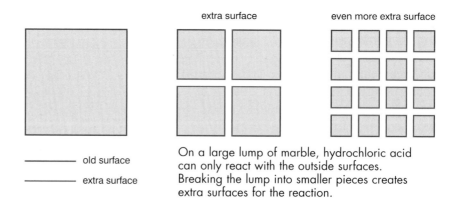

---------- old surface

---------- extra surface

On a large lump of marble, hydrochloric acid can only react with the outside surfaces. Breaking the lump into smaller pieces creates extra surfaces for the reaction.

Catalysts

Adding a catalyst speeds up the rate of a chemical reaction, and catalysts are chemically unchanged at the end of the reaction.

An example is manganese(IV) oxide which increases the rate of decomposition of hydrogen peroxide to water and oxygen.

QUESTIONS

Q1 For a chemical reaction to occur the reacting particles must collide. Why don't all collisions between the particles of the reactants lead to a chemical reaction?

Q2 The diagrams (right) show the activation energies of two different reactions A and B. Which reaction is likely to have the greater rate of reaction at a particular temperature?

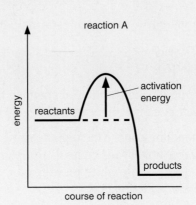
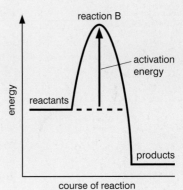

Q3 Look at the table of results obtained when dilute hydrochloric acid is added to marble chips.

Time (seconds)	0	10	20	30	40	50	60	70	80	90
Volume of gas (cm^3)	0	20	36	49	58	65	69	70	70	70

  a What is the name of the gas produced in this reaction?

  b Use the results to calculate the volume of gas produced:
    i in the first 10 seconds
    ii between 10 and 20 seconds
    iii between 20 and 30 seconds
    iv between 80 and 90 seconds.

  c Explain how your answers to part b show that the rate of reaction decreases as the reaction proceeds.

  d Use collision theory to explain why the rate of reaction decreases as the reaction proceeds.

  e In this experiment the rate of the reaction was followed by measuring the volume of gas produced every 10 seconds. What alternative measurement could have been used?

Q4 Why does increasing the temperature increase the rate of a reaction?

Q5 The graph shows the results obtained in three different experiments. In each experiment marble chips were added to 50 cm^3 of 1 mol dm^{-3} hydrochloric acid (in excess) at room temperature. The same mass of marble was used each time but different sized chips were used in each experiment.

  a i In which experiment was the reaction the fastest?
    ii Give a reason for your answer.

  b i Which experiment used the largest marble chips?
    ii Give a reason for your answer.

  c i How long did it take for the reaction in experiment 2 to finish?
    ii Why did the reaction finish?

  d Why was the same mass of carbon dioxide lost in each experiment?

  e Experiment 3 was repeated at 50°C rather than room temperature. How would the results be different from those shown for experiment 3?

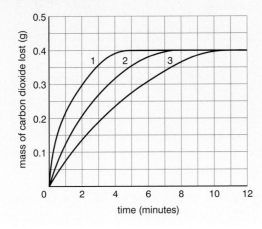

More questions on the CD ROM

EQUILIBRIA

Videos & questions on the CD ROM

Types of reversible reaction

Carbon burns in oxygen to form carbon dioxide:

carbon	+	oxygen	→	carbon dioxide
C(s)	+	$O_2(g)$	→	$CO_2(g)$

Carbon dioxide cannot be changed back into carbon and oxygen. The reaction cannot be reversed.

When blue copper(II) sulphate crystals are heated, a white powder is formed (anhydrous copper(II) sulphate) and water is lost as steam. If water is added to this white powder, blue copper(II) sulphate is re-formed. The reaction is **reversible**:

copper(II) sulphate crystals	⇌	anhydrous copper(II) sulphate	+	water
$CuSO_4.5H_2O(s)$	⇌	$CuSO_4(s)$	+	$5H_2O(l)$

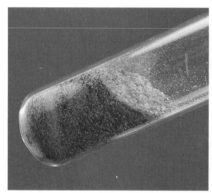  

When copper(II) sulphate crystals are heated they turn from blue to white.

The reaction can then be reversed by adding water.

A* EXTRA

- A chemical equilibrium is an example of a dynamic equilibrium (a moving equilibrium). Reactants are constantly forming products, and products are constantly reforming the reactants. Equilibrium is reached when the rates of the forward and backward reactions are the same.

A reversible reaction can go from left to right or from right to left – notice the double-headed '⇌' arrow used when writing these equations.

Another reversible reaction is the reaction between ethene and water to make ethanol. This is one of the reactions used industrially to make ethanol:

ethene	+	water	⇌	ethanol
$C_2H_4(g)$	+	$H_2O(g)$	⇌	$C_2H_5OH(g)$

When ethene and water are heated in the presence of a catalyst in a sealed container, ethanol is produced.

As the ethene and water are used up, the rate of the forward reaction decreases. As the amount of ethanol increases the rate of the back reaction (the decomposition of ethanol) increases. Eventually the rate of formation of ethanol will exactly equal the rate of decomposition of ethanol. The amounts of ethene, water and ethanol will be constant. The reaction is said to be in **equilibrium**.

Changing the position of equilibrium

Reversible reactions can be a nuisance to an industrial chemist. You want to make a particular product but as soon as it forms it starts to change back into the reactants! Fortunately scientists have found ways of increasing the amount of product that can be obtained (the **yield**) in a reversible reaction by moving the position of balance to favour the products rather than the reactants.

The position of equilibrium or yield can be changed in the following ways:
- changing **concentrations**
- changing **pressure**
- changing **temperature**.

In the following example:

$$A(g) + 2B(g) \rightleftharpoons 2C(g) \qquad \Delta H = +$$

The yield of C is *increased* by:

1 adding more A and B
removing C $\Big\}$ concentration

2 increasing the **pressure** because there are 3 molecules on the left (high pressure) but only 2 molecules on the right (low pressure)

3 increasing the **temperature** because the reaction is endothermic (ΔH is +).

A **catalyst** increases the rate at which the equilibrium is achieved. It does not change the yield because it does not affect the position of the equilibrium.

QUESTIONS

Q1 When a chemical reaction is in equilibrium what does this mean?

Q2 What effect does a catalyst have on:
a the rate of reaction
b the yield of a reaction?

More questions on the CD ROM

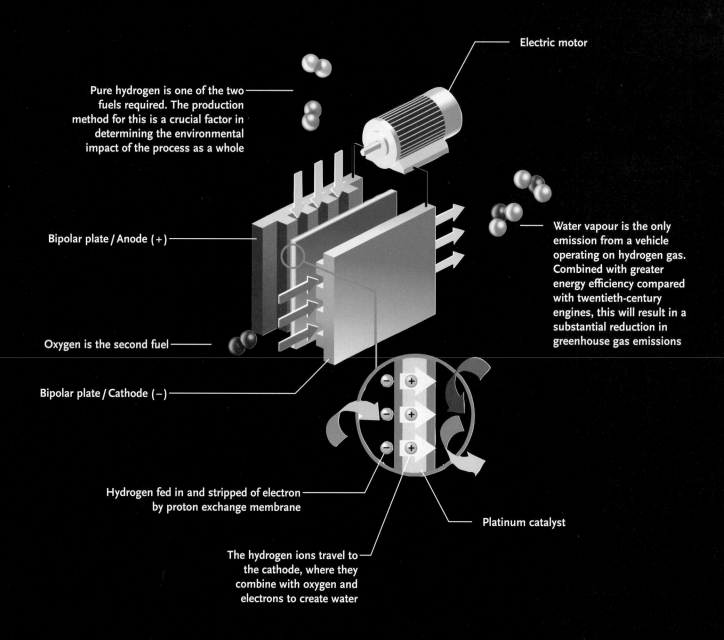

Electric motor

Pure hydrogen is one of the two fuels required. The production method for this is a crucial factor in determining the environmental impact of the process as a whole

Water vapour is the only emission from a vehicle operating on hydrogen gas. Combined with greater energy efficiency compared with twentieth-century engines, this will result in a substantial reduction in greenhouse gas emissions

Bipolar plate / Anode (+)

Oxygen is the second fuel

Bipolar plate / Cathode (−)

Hydrogen fed in and stripped of electron by proton exchange membrane

Platinum catalyst

The hydrogen ions travel to the cathode, where they combine with oxygen and electrons to create water

You are the Future

Hundreds of chemical reactions are going on in your body as you're reading this, just as they are everywhere else in the world. If you upset the natural balance – perhaps by eating or drinking the wrong thing – chemistry can put things right. We call it medicine.

We are just one part of the world; but what we do affects the whole planet. The chemistry that drives our modern lives – fertilisers, plastics, transport – is also polluting our earth. It doesn't have to be like that.

Future chemists – especially in regions like parts of Asia where industry is comparatively new – have a real chance to develop new, cleaner processes instead of repeating the mistakes of the

Chapter 5

CHEMISTRY IN SOCIETY

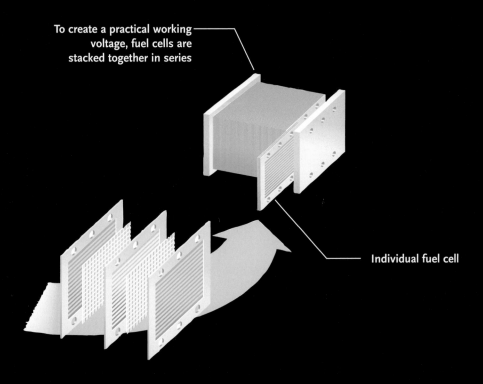

To create a practical working
voltage, fuel cells are
stacked together in series

Individual fuel cell

THE EXTRACTION AND USES OF METALS

How are metals extracted?

Metals are found in the form of **ores** containing **minerals** mixed with unwanted rock. In almost all cases, the mineral is a compound of the metal, not the pure metal. One exception is gold, which exists naturally in a pure state.

Extracting a metal from its ore usually involves two steps:
1 The mineral is physically separated from unwanted rock
2 The mineral is chemically broken down to obtain the metal.

Reactivity of metals

The chemical method chosen to break down a mineral depends on the reactivity of the metal. The **more reactive** a metal is, the **harder** it is to break down its compounds. The more reactive metals are obtained from their minerals by the process of **electrolysis**.

The less reactive metals can be obtained by heating their oxides with carbon. This method will only work for metals below carbon in the **reactivity series**. It involves the **reduction** of a metal oxide to the metal.

Metal	Extraction method
potassium sodium calcium magnesium aluminium	The most reactive metals are obtained using electrolysis.
(carbon)	
zinc iron tin lead copper	These metals are below carbon in the reactivity series and so can be obtained by heating their oxides with carbon.
silver gold	The least reactive metals are found as pure elements.

Extracting aluminium

Aluminium is extracted from the ore **bauxite**. The aluminium oxide is extracted from bauxite by a purification process. The aluminium oxide is insoluble, so it is **melted** to allow the ions to move when an electric current is passed through it. The anodes are made from carbon and the cathode is the carbon-lined steel case.

At the cathode **aluminium** is formed:

aluminium ions	+	electrons	$\rightarrow$	aluminium
$Al^{3+}(l)$	+	$3e^-$	$\rightarrow$	$Al(l)$

At the anode **oxygen** is formed:

oxide ions	$\rightarrow$	oxygen molecules	+	electrons
$2O^{2-}(l)$	$\rightarrow$	$O_2(g)$	+	$4e^-$

The oxygen reacts with the carbon anodes to form carbon dioxide.
The rods constantly need to be replaced because of this. This process uses
very large quantities of electricity and to be economical needs low-price
electricity. Aluminium is often extracted in countries with plentiful supplies
of hydroelectric power.

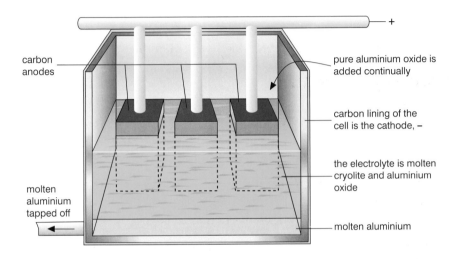

carbon anodes

pure aluminium oxide is added continually

carbon lining of the cell is the cathode, –

the electrolyte is molten cryolite and aluminium oxide

molten aluminium tapped off

molten aluminium

The extraction of aluminium is expensive. The aluminium oxide is added to the cryolite to lower the melting point and save energy costs.

Using carbon to extract metals

Copper is extracted by heating the mineral **malachite** (copper(II)
carbonate) with carbon. The reaction takes place in two stages:

Stage 1 – The malachite decomposes:

copper(II) carbonate	$\rightarrow$	copper(II) oxide	+	carbon dioxide
$CuCO_3(s)$	$\rightarrow$	$CuO(s)$	+	$CO_2(g)$

Stage 2 – The copper(II) oxide is reduced by the carbon:

copper(II) oxide	+	carbon	$\rightarrow$	copper	+	carbon dioxide
$2CuO(s)$	+	$C(s)$	$\rightarrow$	$2Cu(s)$	+	$CO_2(g)$

The copper produced by this process is purified by electrolysis.

Iron, lead and zinc are also extracted in large quantities by heating their
oxides with carbon. Metals that are above carbon in the reactivity series
cannot be obtained by heating their oxides with carbon.

The blast furnace

Iron is produced on a very large scale by reduction using carbon. The reaction takes place in a huge furnace called a **blast furnace**.

Three important raw materials are put in the top of the furnace: **iron ore** (iron(III) oxide, the source of iron), **coke** (the source of carbon needed for the reduction) and **limestone**, needed to remove the impurities as a 'slag'.

Coke, iron ore, limestone

Molten iron

Slag

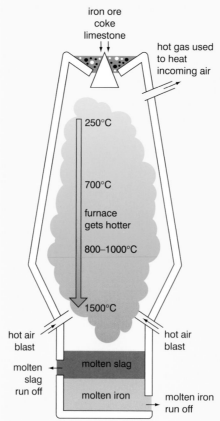

iron ore
coke
limestone

hot gas used to heat incoming air

250°C

700°C

furnace gets hotter

800–1000°C

1500°C

hot air blast

hot air blast

molten slag run off

molten slag

molten iron

molten iron run off

1 Iron ore, coke and limestone are fed into the top of the blast furnace

2 Hot air is blasted up the furnace from the bottom

3 Oxygen from the air reacts with coke to form carbon dioxide:
$$C(s) + O_2(g) \longrightarrow CO_2(g)$$

4 Carbon dioxide reacts with more coke to form carbon monoxide:
$$CO_2(g) + C(s) \longrightarrow 2CO(g)$$

5 Carbon monoxide is a reducing agent. Iron(III) oxide is reduced to iron:
reduction = loss of oxygen
$$Fe_2O_3(s) + 3CO(g) \longrightarrow 2Fe(l) + 3CO_2(g)$$

6 Dense molten iron runs to the bottom of the furnace and is run off. There are many impurities in iron ore. The limestone helps to remove these as shown in 7 and 8.

7 Limestone is broken down by heat to calcium oxide:
$$CaCO_3(s) \longrightarrow CaO(s) + CO_2(g)$$

8 Calcium oxide reacts with impurities like sand (silicon dioxide) to form a liquid called 'slag':
$$CaO(s) + SiO_2(s) \longrightarrow CaSiO_3(l)$$
impurity   slag
The liquid slag falls to the bottom of the furnace and is tapped off.

The overall reaction is:

iron oxide	+	carbon	$\rightarrow$	iron	+	carbon dioxide
$2Fe_2O_3(s)$	+	$3C$	$\rightarrow$	$4Fe$	+	$3CO_2$

The reduction happens in three stages.

Stage 1 – The coke (carbon) reacts with oxygen 'blasted' into the furnace:

carbon	+	oxygen	$\rightarrow$	carbon dioxide
$C(s)$	+	$O_2(g)$	$\rightarrow$	$CO_2(g)$

Stage 2 – The carbon dioxide is reduced by unreacted coke to form carbon monoxide:

carbon dioxide	+	carbon	$\rightarrow$	carbon monoxide
$CO_2(g)$	+	$C(s)$	$\rightarrow$	$2CO(g)$

Stage 3 – The iron(III) oxide is reduced by the carbon monoxide to iron:

iron(III) oxide	+	carbon monoxide	$\rightarrow$	iron	+	carbon dioxide
$Fe_2O_3(s)$	+	$3CO(g)$	$\rightarrow$	$2Fe(s)$	+	$3CO_2(g)$

Making steel from iron

Iron from the blast furnace is **brittle** and **corrodes** very easily because it contains a large percentage of carbon (from the coke).

The corrosion of iron is called **rusting** and it is a chemical reaction between iron, water and oxygen. Common ways of protecting iron from rusting are:

- **Galvanising** – covering iron in zinc. The zinc corrodes instead of the iron if the coating is damaged. This is called **sacrificial protection**.

- **Alloying** – mixing iron with other metals to make steel.

In **steel making**, the molten iron (pig iron) straight from the blast furnace is heated, and oxygen is passed through it to remove some of the large percentage of carbon present after the iron is extracted:

$$C(s) + O_2(g) \rightarrow CO_2(g)$$

Steel is iron with 0.1–1.5% carbon content. Steel is more resistant to corrosion and is less brittle than iron. It has a wide range of uses, depending on its carbon content. For example:

low carbon (<0.3%) – car bodies
medium carbon (0.3 – 0.9%) – rail tracks
high carbon (0.9 – 1.5%) – knives

Stainless steels are made by adding a wide range of metals to steel such as chromium, nickel, vanadium and cobalt. Each one gives the steel particular properties for specific uses. For example, vanadium steel is used to make high precision, hard-wearing industrial tools.

A* EXTRA

- In a blast furnace the iron(III) oxide is reduced to iron by carbon monoxide, formed when the carbon reacts with the air blasted into the furnace. In the reduction of iron(III) oxide, the carbon monoxide is oxidised to carbon dioxide.

The extraction of zinc

Zinc can be extracted from zinc blende, ZnS or sometimes calamine, $ZnCO_3$.

First zinc oxide is produced by heating

zinc sulphide	+	oxygen	→	zinc oxide	+	sulphur dioxide
$2ZnS(s)$	+	$3O_2(g)$	→	$2ZnO(s)$	+	$2SO_2(g)$

Then the zinc oxide can be treated in one of two possible ways:

Either by reduction in a blast furnace:

zinc oxide	+	carbon monoxide	→	zinc	+	carbon dioxide
$ZnO(s)$	+	$CO(g)$	→	$Zn(l)$ +		$CO_2(g)$

The liquid zinc is then purified using fractional distillation.

Or the oxide is first dissolved in sulphuric acid to make zinc sulphate ions.

$$ZnO(s) + H_2SO_4(aq) \rightarrow ZnSO_4(aq) + H_2O(l)$$

Then the solution of zinc sulphate is electrolysed using a pure zinc cathode and a carbon anode. The half reaction at the cathode is:

$$Zn^{2+}(aq) + 2e^- \rightarrow Zn(s)$$

The extraction of chromium

In the thermite process chromium(III) oxide is heated in an electric arc furnace with silicon and calcium oxide.

chromium oxide	+	silicon	+	calcium oxide	→	chromium	+	calcium silicate
$2Cr_2O_3$	+	$3Si$	+	$3CaO$	→	$4Cr$	+	$3CaSiO_3$

Uses of metals

Metal	Properties	Uses
Aluminium	Aluminium is very light	used in aircraft construction
Iron	Strong and malleable	car bodies, cutlery
Zinc	Zinc has a low melting point so can be coated onto harder metals	used to coat iron to prevent rusting (galvanised iron)
Chromium	Chronium is very strong and resistant to corrosion	used to make stainless steel
Copper	Copper is a very good conductor of electricity	electrical wiring

QUESTIONS

Q1 Iron is made from iron ore (iron oxide) in a blast furnace by heating with carbon.
- **a** Write a word equation for the overall reaction.
- **b** Is the iron oxide oxidised or reduced in this reaction? Explain your answer.
- **c** Why is limestone also added to the blast furnace?

Q2 For any metal, what determines the method of extraction used to obtain it from its ore?

Q3 All methods of extracting metals from their ores are reduction processes. Explain this fact.

Q4 Aluminium is extracted from aluminium oxide (Al_2O_3) by electrolysis. Aluminium oxide contains Al^{3+} and O^{2-} ions. The aluminium oxide is heated until it is in a molten state. Why is the electrolysis carried out on molten rather than solid aluminium oxide?

More questions on the CD ROM

NATURAL GAS AND OIL

What are fossil fuels?

Crude oil, natural gas and coal are **fossil fuels**.

Crude oil was formed millions of years ago from the remains of animals that were pressed together under layers of rock. It is usually found deep underground, trapped between layers of rock that it can't seep through (**impermeable** rock). Natural gas is often trapped in pockets above the crude oil.

The supply of fossil fuels is limited – they are called 'finite' or **non-renewable** fuels. They are an extremely valuable resource which must be used efficiently.

Fossil fuels contain many useful chemicals, and we need to separate these chemicals so that they are not wasted. For example, coal is often converted into coke by removing some of the chemicals in the coal. When the coke is burnt as a fuel, these chemicals are not wasted.

An oil refinery in Malaysia.

Separating the fractions

The chemicals in crude oil are separated into useful **fractions** by a process known as **fractional distillation**.

The fractionating column converts the crude oil into many useful fractions.

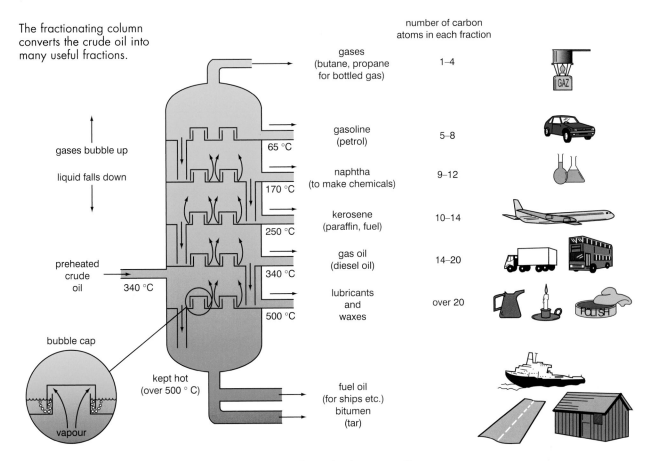

The crude oil is heated in a furnace and passed into the bottom of a **fractionating column**. The vapour mixture given off rises up the column and the different fractions condense out at different parts of the column. The fractions that come off near the top of the column are light-coloured runny liquids. Those removed near the bottom of the column are dark and treacle-like. Thick liquids that are not runny, such as these bottom-most fractions, are described as 'viscous'.

How does fractional distillation work?

The components present in crude oil separate because they have different boiling points. A simple particle model explains why their boiling points differ. Crude oil is a mixture of **hydrocarbon** molecules which contain only carbon and hydrogen. The molecules are chemically bonded in similar ways with strong covalent bonds (see Unit 1), but contain different numbers of carbon atoms.

heptane

octane

Notice that octane has one more carbon atom and two more hydrogen atoms than heptane. Their formulae differ by CH_2.

A* EXTRA

- As a general rule, the greater the surface area for contact, the stronger the force between the molecules.

The weak attractive forces between the molecules have to be broken if the hydrocarbon is to boil. The longer a hydrocarbon molecule is, the stronger the intermolecular forces are between the molecules. The stronger these bonds, the higher the boiling point, since more energy is needed to overcome the larger forces.

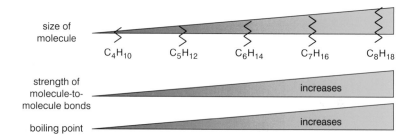

The smaller-molecule hydrocarbons more readily form a vapour – they are more **volatile**. For example, we can smell petrol (with molecules containing between 5 and 10 carbon atoms) much more easily than engine oil (with molecules containing between 14 and 20 carbon atoms) because petrol is more volatile.

Another difference between the fractions is how easily they burn and how smoky their flames are.

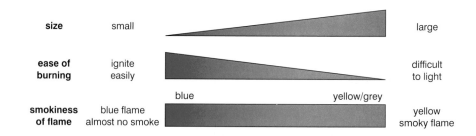

Cracking the oil fractions

The composition of crude oil varies in different parts of the world. The table shows the composition of a sample of crude oil from the Middle East after fractional distillation.

Fraction (in order of increasing boiling point)	Percentage produced by fractional distillation
liquefied petroleum gases (LPG)	3
gasoline	13
naphtha	9
kerosene	12
diesel	14
heavy oils and bitumen	49

The larger molecules can be broken down into smaller ones by **cracking**. Cracking requires a **high temperature** and a **catalyst**.

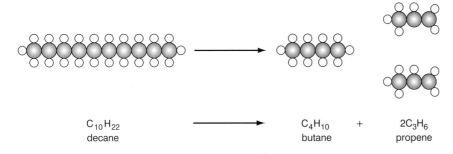

C$_{10}$H$_{22}$ C$_4$H$_{10}$ +   2C$_3$H$_6$
decane   butane   propene

The decane molecule (C$_{10}$H$_{22}$) is converted into the smaller molecules butane (C$_4$H$_{10}$) and propene (C$_3$H$_6$).

The butane and propene formed in this example of cracking have different types of structures.

Reforming the molecules from cracking and oil fractions

Reforming is a process in which the **straight-chain** molecules are broken into smaller molecules which are then re-joined to form **branched-chain** molecules.

C$_8$H$_{18}$
octane

reforming

CH$_3$CH(CH$_3$)CH(CH$_3$)CH(CH$_3$)CH$_3$
2,3,4-trimethylpentane

The straight-chain octane molecule is reformed into a branched-chain molecule, 2,3,4-trimethylpentane.

The purpose of doing this is to make **high grade petrol**. The petrol fraction is a mixture of branched-chain and straight-chain molecules. Straight-chain molecules catch fire more easily than branched-chain molecules. For petrol to work efficiently, it needs to burn in the combustion chamber with oxygen at the correct temperature. This is why high-grade petrol is made of branched-chain molecules with only a few straight-chain molecules.

Combustion of fuels

Most of the common fuels used today are hydrocarbons – substances that contain **only** carbon and hydrogen atoms.

When a hydrocarbon is burnt in a plentiful supply of air it reacts with the oxygen in the air (it is **oxidised**) to form carbon dioxide and water. This reaction is an example of **combustion**.

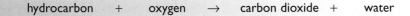

hydrocarbon   +   oxygen   →   carbon dioxide   +   water

For example, when methane (natural gas) is burnt

$$CH_4(g) \quad + \quad 2O_2(g) \quad \rightarrow \quad CO_2(g) \quad + \quad 2H_2O(l)$$

The complete combustion of methane in a plentiful supply of air.

The air contains only about 20% oxygen by volume. When a hydrocarbon fuel is burnt there is not always enough oxygen for complete combustion. Instead, some **incomplete combustion** occurs, forming **carbon** or **carbon monoxide**:

methane	+	oxygen	→	carbon monoxide	+	water
$2CH_4(g)$	+	$3O_2(g)$	→	$2CO(g)$	+	$4H_2O(l)$
methane	+	oxygen	→	carbon	+	water
$CH_4(g)$	+	$O_2(g)$	→	$C(s)$	+	$2H_2O(l)$

Incomplete combustion is **costly** because the full energy content of the fuel is not being released and the formation of carbon or soot reduces the efficiency of the burner being used. It can be **dangerous** as carbon monoxide is extremely poisonous. Carbon monoxide molecules attach to the haemoglobin of the blood, preventing oxygen from doing so. Brain cells deprived of their supply of oxygen will quickly die.

The tell-tale sign that a fuel is burning incompletely is that the flame is **yellow**. When complete combustion occurs the flame will be **blue**.

Problems from transporting crude oil

It is still cheap to **transport** large cargoes by sea, e.g. grain and crude oil, and the number of merchant ships and tankers continues to rise. Occasionally, ships do have accidents and shed their cargoes. When a tanker carrying **crude oil** has a spill, it causes enormous environmental damage, especially if near land where it washes to shore and affects birds and other sea life.

After an oil spill at sea, a thin layer of oil covers a large area of the surface. If allowed to spread, it **prevents evaporation** of water and so affects the water cycle. Hydrocarbons being released into the atmosphere can cause damage to the environment.

Burning hydrocarbon fuels produces carbon dioxide, water and nitrogen oxides. These contribute to global warming and acid rain. Hydrocarbons can also harm the environment if they are released 'unburnt', which happens in small amounts in most engines. These hydrocarbons help to form smog in the atmosphere. Chemical reactions between the hydrocarbons, stimulated by UV light, create photochemical smog. The smog reacts with ozone in the upper levels of the atmosphere. Ozone helps to protect the Earth from dangerous UV light. The hydrocarbons react with the ozone to create a thinning of the layer, letting more light through, leading to an increase in skin cancer and a reduction of productivity of some crop plants.

QUESTIONS

Q1 a How was crude oil formed?

b Why is crude oil a non-renewable fuel?

Q2 The diagram shows a column used to separate the components present in crude oil.

a Name the process used to separate crude oil into fractions.

b What happens to the boiling point of the mixture as it goes up the column?

c The mixture of vapours arrives at level X. What now happens to the various parts of the mixture?

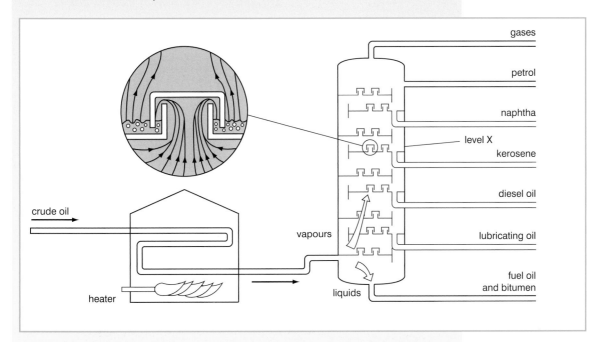

Q3 The cracking of decane molecules is shown by the equation
$C_{10}H_{22} \rightarrow Y + C_2H_4$

a Decane is a hydrocarbon. What is a hydrocarbon?

b What conditions are needed for cracking?

c Write down the molecular formula for hydrocarbon Y.

Q4 How can oil spillage from tankers at sea affect the 'water cycle' of Earth?

Q5 a Petrol is a hydrocarbon. Write a word equation for the reaction when petrol burns in a plentiful supply of air.

b When petrol is burnt in a car engine, carbon monoxide may be formed.
What condition causes the formation of carbon monoxide?

c Explain what effect carbon monoxide has on the body.

More questions on the CD ROM

SYNTHETIC POLYMERS

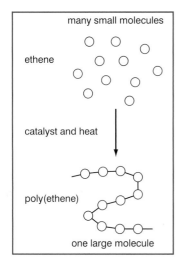

many small molecules

ethene

catalyst and heat

poly(ethene)

one large molecule

Ethene molecules link together to produce a long polymer chain of poly(ethene).

Addition polymerisation

Alkenes can be used to make **polymers** which are very large molecules made up of many identical smaller molecules called **monomers**. Alkenes are able to react with themselves. They join together into long chains like adding beads to a necklace. When the monomers add together like this the material produced is called an **addition polymer**. Poly(ethene) or polythene is made this way.

By changing the atoms or groups of atoms attached to the carbon–carbon double bond, a whole range of different polymers can be made:

Plastics are very difficult to dispose of. Most of them are not **biodegradable** – they cannot be decomposed by bacteria in the soil. Currently, most waste plastic material is buried in landfill sites or is burnt, but burning plastics produces toxic fumes and landfill sites are filling up.

Some types of plastic can be melted down and used again. These are **thermoplastics**. Other types of plastic decompose when they are heated. These are **thermosetting** plastics. Recycling is difficult because the different types of plastic must be separated.

Name of monomer	Displayed formula of monomer	Name of polymer	Displayed formula of polymer	Uses of polymer
ethene	$\begin{array}{c} H \quad\quad H \\ \backslash \quad\quad / \\ C=C \\ / \quad\quad \backslash \\ H \quad\quad H \end{array}$	poly(ethene)	$\left(\begin{array}{c} H \quad H \\ \mid \quad\; \mid \\ C-C \\ \mid \quad\; \mid \\ H \quad H \end{array}\right)_n$	buckets, bowls, plastic bags
chloroethene (vinyl chloride)	$\begin{array}{c} H \quad\quad H \\ \backslash \quad\quad / \\ C=C \\ / \quad\quad \backslash \\ Cl \quad\quad H \end{array}$	poly(chloroethene) (polyvinylchloride)	$\left(\begin{array}{c} H \quad H \\ \mid \quad\; \mid \\ C-C \\ \mid \quad\; \mid \\ Cl \quad H \end{array}\right)_n$	plastic sheets, artificial leather
phenylethene (styrene)	$\begin{array}{c} H \quad\quad H \\ \backslash \quad\quad / \\ C=C \\ / \quad\quad \backslash \\ C_6H_5 \quad H \end{array}$	poly(phenylethene) (polystyrene)	$\left(\begin{array}{c} H \quad H \\ \mid \quad\; \mid \\ C-C \\ \mid \quad\; \mid \\ C_6H_5 \; H \end{array}\right)_n$	yoghurt cartons, packaging
tetrafluoroethene	$\begin{array}{c} F \quad\quad F \\ \backslash \quad\quad / \\ C=C \\ / \quad\quad \backslash \\ F \quad\quad F \end{array}$	poly(tetrafluroethene) or PTFE	$\left(\begin{array}{c} F \quad F \\ \mid \quad\; \mid \\ C-C \\ \mid \quad\; \mid \\ F \quad F \end{array}\right)_n$	non-stick coating in frying pans

In thermoplastics the intermolecular forces are weak and break on heating. The plastic can be melted and re-moulded. In thermosetting plastics the intermolecular bonds are strong interlinking covalent bonds. The whole structure breaks down when these bonds are broken by heating.

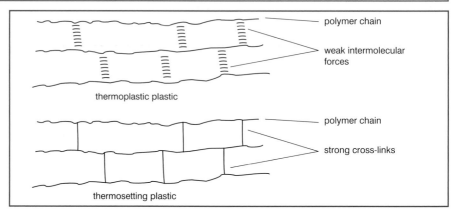

polymer chain

weak intermolecular forces

thermoplastic plastic

polymer chain

strong cross-links

thermosetting plastic

Condensation polymerisation

Polymers can also be made by joining together two different monomers so that they react together. When they react they expel a small molecule in the process. Because the small molecule is usually water the process is called **condensation polymerisation**.

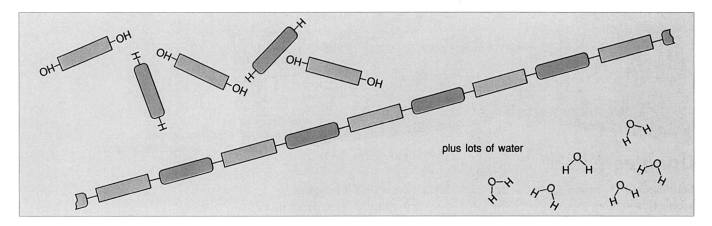

plus lots of water

The manufacture of nylon

The starting monomers for nylon are called 1,6-diaminohexane and hexanedioic acid.

When the monomers react together they make an amide link, so nylon is called a polyamide.

$$H_2N(CH_2)_6NH_2 \;+\; HOOC(CH_2)_4COOH \;\rightarrow$$

$$H_2N(CH_2)_6NHOC(CH_2)_4COOH \;+\; H_2O$$

The central portion of the polymer is an **amide link**.

$$\begin{matrix} H & O \\ | & || \\ -N- & C- \end{matrix}$$

The structure of nylon can be shown in a block diagram:

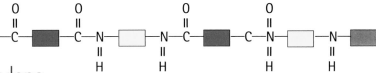

The manufacture of terylene

Terylene is also a condensation polymer and it is made the same way as nylon. This time the starting reactants are ethane-1,2-diol and benzene-1,4-dicarboxylic acid.

When the polymer is formed the linkage is an ester linkage: Because of the ester linkage, terylene is called a **polyester**.

$$\begin{matrix} & O \\ & || \\ -O- & C- \end{matrix}$$

QUESTIONS

Q1 a Draw the displayed formula for propene.
  b Write an equation using displayed formulae to show how propene can be polymerised.
  c What is the name of the polymer formed in b?
  d Explain why propane cannot form polymers as propene does.

Q2 What is meant by the words **monomer** and **polymer**?

More questions on the CD ROM

THE MANUFACTURE OF SOME IMPORTANT CHEMICALS

The manufacture of ammonia

Ammonia is used to make nitrogen-containing fertilisers.

It is manufactured in the **Haber process** from nitrogen and hydrogen. The conditions include an iron catalyst, a temperature of 450 °C and 200 times atmospheric pressure.

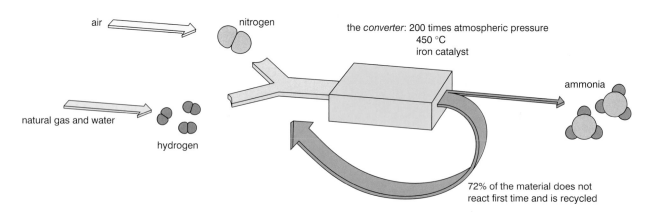

The Haber Process for making ammonia. The reactants have to be recycled to increase the amount of ammonia produced.

nitrogen	+	hydrogen	⇌	ammonia	
$N_2(g)$	+	$3H_2(g)$	⇌	$2NH_3(g)$	$\Delta H = -92$ kJ mol^{-1}

The greatest yield of ammonia would be made using a low temperature (it is exothermic) but this would be slow. The temperature used of 450 °C is a compromise since not so much is made, but it is produced faster. The iron catalyst is used to increase the rate also – it does not increase the yield. High pressure increases the yield and also the rate.

The graph shows the effect of temperature and pressure on the yield of ammonia.

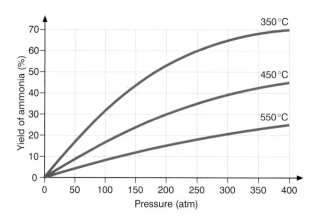

Effect of temperature and pressure on yield of ammonia.

Ammonia is used for the manufacture of nitric acid and to make NPK fertilisers. NPK means the fertiliser contains nitrogen, phosphorus and potassium.

The manufacture of nitric acid from ammonia

Nitric acid is manufactured by the Ostwald process.

First ammonia is oxidised to make nitrogen monoxide.

A mixture of purified air and ammonia gas is passed through a platinum-rhodium gauze at 850°C. The metal gauze is a catalyst.

ammonia	+	oxygen	$\rightarrow$	nitrogen monoxide	+	water
$4NH_3(g)$	+	$5O_2(g)$	$\rightarrow$	$4NO(g)$	+	$6H_2O(g)$

In the second stage the nitrogen monoxide is cooled and mixed with air to make nitrogen dioxide.

nitrogen monoxide	+	oxygen	$\rightarrow$	nitrogen dioxide
$2NO(g)$	+	$O_2(g)$	$\rightarrow$	$2NO_2(g)$

In the third stage the nitrogen dioxide is dissolved in water to make the nitric acid.

nitrogen dioxide	+	oxygen	$\rightarrow$	nitric acid	+	water
$4NO_2(g)$	+	$O_2(g)$	$\rightarrow$	$4HNO_3(aq)$	+	$2H_2O(l)$

The manufacture of sulphuric acid

Sulphur can be found in nature in underground beds. It also occurs in metal ores and can be recovered from natural gas and oil.

Sulphuric acid is a very important starting material in the chemical industry. It is used in the manufacture of many other chemicals, from fertilisers to plastics.

It is manufactured in a process known as the **contact process** – sulphur dioxide is oxidised to sulphur trioxide.

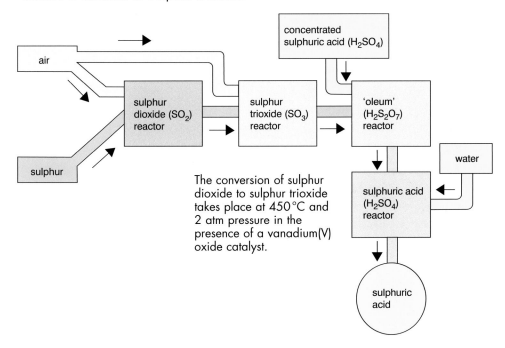

The conversion of sulphur dioxide to sulphur trioxide takes place at 450°C and 2 atm pressure in the presence of a vanadium(V) oxide catalyst.

The equations for the steps in making sulphuric acid are:

1 sulphur + oxygen → sulphur dioxide
$S(s)$ + $O_2(g)$ → $SO_2(g)$

2 sulphur dioxide + oxygen $\rightleftharpoons$ sulphur trioxide
$2SO_2(g)$ + $O_2(g)$ $\rightleftharpoons$ $2SO_3(g)$ $\Delta H = -192 \text{ kJ mol}^{-1}$

3 sulphur trioxide + sulphuric acid → 'oleum'
(concentrated)
$SO_3(g)$ + $H_2SO_4(l)$ → $H_2S_2O_7(l)$

4 'oleum' + water → sulphuric acid
$H_2S_2O_7(l)$ + $H_2O(l)$ → $2H_2SO_4(l)$

It would seem simpler to make sulphuric acid by adding sulphur trioxide straight to water to avoid steps 3 and 4:

$H_2O(l) + SO_3(g) \rightarrow H_2SO_4(l)$

This is dangerous because the reaction is very exothermic and an 'acid mist' is made.

Step 2 above is the reaction of the contact process. The greatest yield of sulphur trioxide would be made at a low temperature (the reaction is exothermic), but this would be slow, so the compromise temperature of 450 °C is used – less is made but in a shorter time. High pressure would make more SO_3 but the equipment required would be costly. A catalyst increases the rate but not the yield.

Acid rain

Sulphur dioxide and nitrogen oxides are pollutant gases which contribute to acid rain.

Burning fossil fuels gives off many gases, including **sulphur dioxide** and various **nitrogen oxides**.

sulphur + oxygen → sulphur dioxide
$S(s)$ + $O_2(g)$ → $SO_2(g)$

Sulphur dioxide combines with water to form sulphuric acid. Nitrogen oxide combines with water to form nitric acid. These substances can make the rain acidic (called **acid rain**).

sulphur dioxide + oxygen + water → sulphuric acid
$2SO_2(g)$ + $O_2(g)$ + $2H_2O(l)$ → $2H_2SO_4(aq)$

Buildings, particularly those made of limestone and marble (both are forms of calcium carbonate, $CaCO_3$), are damaged by acid rain. Metal structures are also attacked by sulphuric acid.

Acid rain **harms plants** that take in the acidic water and the **animals** that live in the affected rivers and lakes. Acid rain also washes ions such as calcium and magnesium out of the soil, **depleting the minerals available to plants**. It also washes **aluminium**, which is poisonous to fish, out of the soil and into rivers and lakes.

Reducing emission of the gases causing acid rain is expensive, and part of the problem is that the acid rain usually falls a long way from the places where the gases were given off.

Power stations are now being fitted with 'flue gas desulphurisation plants' (FGD), to reduce the release of sulphur dioxide into the atmosphere.

Catalytic converters fitted to vehicles reduce oxides of nitrogen to oxygen and nitrogen.

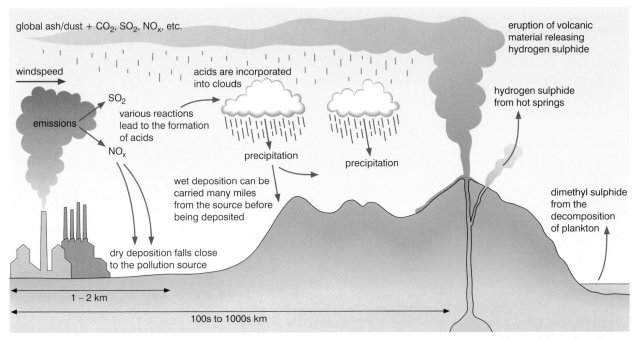

The problem of acid rain.

The manufacture of sodium hydroxide and chlorine

Sodium chloride, NaCl, is the best known of all the 'salt family' and is the reason it is known as **common salt**. From earliest times it has been used to preserve and flavour foodstuffs.

The human body needs a minimum amount of salt to maintain **health**.

Sodium chloride is found in the **oceans** and **seas** and in **land deposits** which were once covered by the oceans.

Solid sodium chloride is **extracted** in three main ways:

1 In hotter climates, **sea water** is poured into large flat open tanks and the heat from the sun **evaporates** off the water.

Land deposits are underground and the salt is obtained in the following ways.

2 The solid salt is **mined** and dug out, then purified by dissolving it in water to produce sodium chloride solution, called **brine**.

3 It is obtained by **solution mining** if the deposits are deep under the ground.

Solution mining.

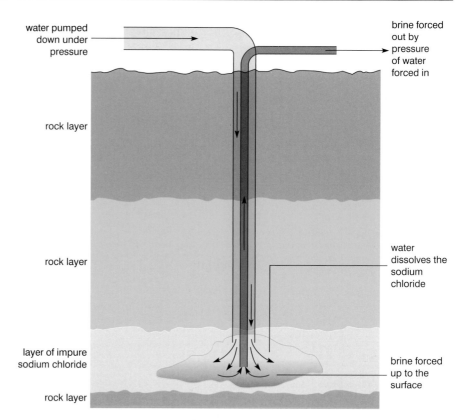

anode   cathode

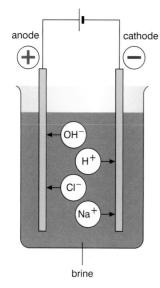

brine

The electrolysis of sodium
chloride solution (brine).

A* EXTRA

- The fact that there are
four ions involved in
sodium chloride
solution, yet in
electrolysis only two
ions are converted to
atoms, is called
preferential discharge.
- You will need to
remember the two ions
that are discharged
and that oxidation and
reduction are involved:
$2Cl^-(aq) \rightarrow Cl_2(g) + 2e^-$ = oxidation of Cl^-

$2H^+(aq) + 2e^- \rightarrow H_2(g)$ = reduction of H^+

What happens when sodium chloride solution (brine) is electrolysed?

When sodium chloride dissolves in water, its **ions** separate:

$NaCl(aq) \rightarrow Na^+(aq) + Cl^-(aq)$

There are also some ions from the water:

$H_2O(l) \rightleftharpoons H^+(aq) + OH^-(aq)$

In the process of **electrolysis**, ions are converted to atoms. In the case of brine:

Na^+ and H^+ are attracted to the cathode (−)

Cl^- and OH^- are attracted to the anode (+).

At the cathode (−)
Sodium is more reactive than hydrogen, so only the **hydrogen ions** are changed to atoms to form a molecule:

$2H^+(aq) + 2e^- \rightarrow H_2(g)$

At the anode (+)
Both OH^- and Cl^- are attracted to the anode, but only the **chloride ions** are changed to atoms to form a molecule:

$2Cl^-(aq) \rightarrow Cl_2(g) + 2e^-$

The remaining solution contains the ions Na^+ and OH^-, so it is sodium hydroxide solution, NaOH(aq).

Summary   At the cathode: hydrogen gas
              At the anode: chlorine gas
              The solution: sodium hydroxide

The electrolysis of brine is a very important industrial process and is the basis of the **chlor–alkali industry,** which is the large-scale production of chlorine, hydrogen and sodium hydroxide.

The chlor-alkali industry

The large-scale manufacture of chlorine, hydrogen and sodium hydroxide by the electrolysis of brine involves collecting the three substances and ensuring *they do not mix together* as they are produced in the electrolytic cell.

The **membrane cell**

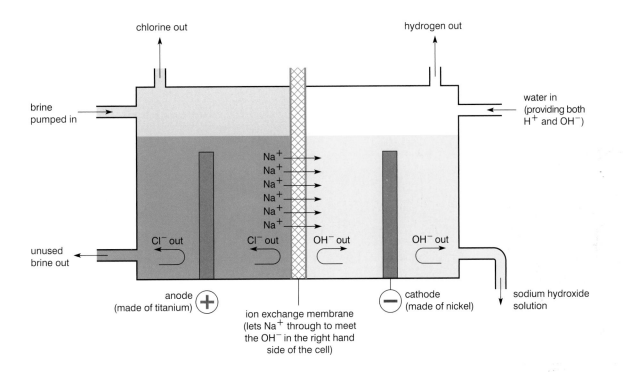

Both chlorine and sodium hydroxide are vitally important chemicals for many industries world-wide in the manufacture of other substances and millions of tonnes of them are used every year . However they are extremely hazardous substances – chlorine was one of the poisonous gases used in World War 1 (1914-18) in 'trench-warfare' to 'gas' enemy troops. Sodium hydroxide is the commonest cheap alkali and called 'caustic soda' – caustic means ' burning' and this is the effect it has on your skin. It is a common misconception that acids are more dangerous than alkalis. Protective gloves should always be worn when handling acids or alkalis (like sodium hydroxide).

A* EXTRA

- The reason for keeping the chlorine and sodium hydroxide apart in the membrane cell is because they react together to form sodium chlorate(I), NaOCl (used as a bleach). You need to comment on this fact to gain a mark and give the formula, NaOCl.

What are the uses of the products of the chlor-alkali industry?

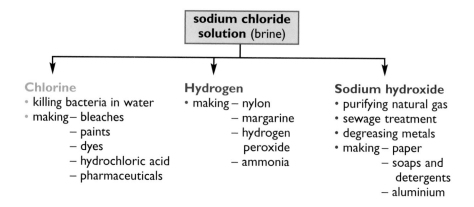

sodium chloride solution (brine)

Chlorine
- killing bacteria in water
- making – bleaches
  - paints
  - dyes
  - hydrochloric acid
  - pharmaceuticals

Hydrogen
- making – nylon
  - margarine
  - hydrogen peroxide
  - ammonia

Sodium hydroxide
- purifying natural gas
- sewage treatment
- degreasing metals
- making – paper
  - soaps and detergents
  - aluminium

QUESTIONS

Q1 In the Haber process for making ammonia the forward reaction is favoured by a low temperature. Why is a temperature as high as 450°C used?

Q2 In the production of sulphuric acid, why is the sulphur trioxide from the contact process not added straight to water to make sulphuric acid?

Q3 a Explain the cause of acid rain.
b Give two effects of acid rain

Q4 The electrolysis of molten sodium chloride produces different products from the electrolysis of aqueous sodium chloride (brine). Write the ionic half equations for the electrolysis of molten sodium chloride at:
a the cathode
b the anode

Q5 a Write the reactions taking place at the cathode and anode in the electrolysis of sodium chloride solution (brine).
b Explain how sodium hydroxide solution is formed during the electrolysis of brine.

Q6 Where does the term 'chlor-alkali' come from?

Q7 Why is it important to keep the products of the electrolysis of brine apart in the industrial electrolytic cells?

Q8 For each gas, give the chemical test used to identify it, and give one large-scale use for it:
a chlorine
b hydrogen.

More questions on the CD ROM

EXAM PRACTICE

I (a) The diagram show the arrangement of particles in the three states of matter. Each circle represents a particle.

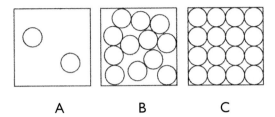

| A | B | C |

Use the letters A, B, and C to give the starting and finishing states of matter of each of the changes in the table.

Change	Starting state	Finishing state		
The formation of water vapour from a puddle of water on a hot day	B	A	✓	①
The formation of solid iron from molten iron	B	C	✓	①
The manufacture of poly(ethene) from ethene	C	A	✗	
The reaction whose equation is ammonium chloride(s) → ammonia(g) + hydrogen chloride(g)	C	A	✓	①

[4]

(b) Which state of matter is the **least** common for the elements of the Periodic Table at room temperature?

gases ✗ _____ [4]

(c) The manufacture of sulphuric acid can be summarised by the equation
$2S(s) + 3O_2(g) + 2H_2O(l) \rightarrow 2H_2SO_4(l)$

Tick one box in each line to show whether the formulae in the table represent a compound, an element or a mixture.

	Compound	Element	Mixture		
$2S(s)$		✔		✓	①
$2S(s) + 3O_2(g)$		✔		✗	
$3O_2(g) + 2H_2O(l)$			✔	✓	①
$2H_2SO_4(l)$	✔			✓	①

[4]

[Total 9 marks]

HOW TO SCORE FULL MARKS

a) It is important to identify the states of matter:

A = gas   B = liquid   C = solid

1. Correct – evaporation process
2. Correct – solidifying
3. Incorrect – should be 'AC' order because ethene is a gas, poly(ethene) a solid
4. Correct – equation shows solid $\rightarrow$ gases (sublimation)

b) Answer is 'liquids'. In the periodic table the majority of elements are solids, a few are gasesbut only two are liquids, i.e. mercury and bromine.

c) 1. Correct – sulphur
2. Incorrect – this is a 'mixture' of two elements.
3. Correct – a mixture of an element (O2) and a compound (H2O)
4. Correct – sulphuric acid

The answers rely on using the state symbols for the equation and a thorough knowledge of the terms: elements, mixtures and compounds.

QUESTION TO TRY (FOUNDATION TIER)

1 (a) Some elements combine together to form ionic compounds. use words from the box to complete the sentences.

Each word may be used once, more than once or not at all.

gained	high	lost	low
medium	metals	non-metals	shared

Ionic compounds are formed between _____ and _____

Electrons are _____ by atoms of one element and

_____ by atoms of the other element.

The ionic compound formed has a _____ melting point and

a _____ boiling point.   [6]

(b) Two elements react to form and ionic compound with the formula $MgCl_2$.

(i) Give the electronic configurations of the two elements in this compound **before** the reaction.

_____ [2]

(ii) Give the electronic configurations of the two elements in this compound **after** the reaction.

_____ [2]

More questions on the CD ROM

[Total 10 marks]

EXAM QUESTION AND STUDENT'S ANSWER (ALTERNATIVE TO COURSEWORK)

1 Solutions of lead(II) nitrate and potassium iodide react together to make the insoluble substance lead(II) iodide.

The equation for the reaction is

$$Pb(NO_3)_2(aq) + 2KI(aq) \rightarrow 2KNO_3(aq) + PbI_2(s)$$

An investigation was carried out to find how much precipitate formed with different volumes of lead(II) nitrate solution.

A student measured out 15 cm³ of potassium iodide solution using measuring cylinder.
He placed this solution in a clean boiling tube.
Using a clean measuring cylinder, he measured out 2 cm³ of lead(II) nitrate solution (of the same concentration, in mol dm⁻³, as the potassium iodide solution). He added this to the potassium iodide solution.
A cloudy yellow mixture formed and this was left to settle.
The student then measured the height (in cm) of the precipitate using a ruler.

The student repeated the experiment using different volumes of lead(II) nitrate solution. The graph shows the results obtained.

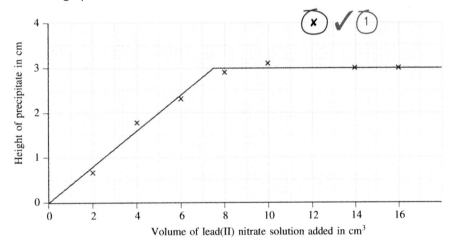

(a) (i) On the graph, circle the point which seems to be anomalous. [1]

(ii) Explain two things that the student may have done in the experiment to give this anomalous result. ①

1 <u>precipitate not settled</u> ✔ <u>because not left long enough</u> ✔ ①

2 _____ [4]

(iii) Why must the graph line go through (0, 0)
<u>cannot have a precipitate if no lead nitrate added yet</u> ✔ ① [1]

(b) Suggest a reason why the height of the precipitate stops increasing.

no more potassium iodide left to react ✔ ①

[1]

(c) (i) How much precipitate has been made in the tube?

solution of soluble salts

precipitate of solid lead(II) iodide

____1.5____ ✔ cm   [1]

(ii) Use the graph to find the volume of lead(II) nitrate solution needed to make this amount of precipitate.

2.9cm³ ✗   [1]

(d) After he had plotted the graph, the student decided he should obtain some more results.

(i) Suggest what volumes of lead(II) nitrate solution he should use.

Between 6cm³ to 10cm³ ✔ ①   [1]

(ii) Explain why he should use these volumes.

Need to know exactly where the graph levels off ✔ ①   [1]

(e) Suggest a different method for measuring the amount of precipitate formed. This method must not be based on the height of the precipitate.

Filter ✔ _off each precipitate and weigh it_ ✔ ①

⑩⁄₁₅   [4]

[Total 15 marks]

HOW TO SCORE FULL MARKS

a) i) Correct point marked.

ii) Correct explanation. Also correct would be adding too much potassium iodide so making more precipitate OR tube not being vertical when being set up so precipitate not level.

iii) Correct response.

b) Correct response – also correct is 'lead(II) nitrate in excess'.

c) i) Correct reading of ruler.

ii) Answer is 3.9 cm^3 – the candidate has misread the horizontal axis scale.

d) i) Correct response.

ii) Correct – this is the purpose of the experiment.

e) 2 marks have been lost here because the filtered-off precipitate needs to be washed (1) and 'dried' (1) before being weighed.

QUESTION TO TRY (ALTERNATIVE TO COURSEWORK)

I Marble chips (calcium carbonate) reacts with hydrochloric acid.

The equation for the reaction is

$$CaCO_3(s) + 2HCl(aq) \rightarrow 2HCl_2(aq) + H_2O(l) + CO_2(g)$$

Some students investigated the rate at which carbon dioxide is given off at 25°C. In separate experiments they used different masses of the same sized marble chips with the same volume of hydrochloric acid (an excess).

(a) The diagram shows the apparatus used. Complete the diagram ot show how the carbon dioxide could be collected and its volume measured.

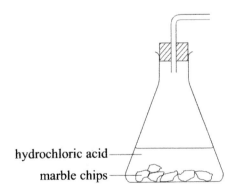

hydrochloric acid

marble chips

[2[

(b) The students recorded these results.

Using 2.34 g of marble chips, 83 cm^3 of carbon dioxide gas were collected in 60 seconds.
We got 45 cm^3 of gas in 1 minute when we used 1.05 g of marble chips.
With 1.47 g of solid we made 98 cm^3 of gas in 120 seconds.
In 60 seconds 0.59 g of solid gave 29 cm^3 of carbon dioxide.
After 90 seconds, 1.21 g of calcium carbonate had made 54 cm^3 of carbon dioxide.

Draw a suitable table and enter all of the results given and the units. [3[

(c) The students' experiment was criticised for not being a **fair test**.
Some students repeated the experiment, making sure it was a fair test.
To do this they measured the volume of gas collected in the first 60 seconds of the reaction.

One student's results are shown own in the table.

Mass of marble chips used (g)	Volume of as collected in 60 seconds (cm³)
0.15	7.5
0.30	17.5
0.60	30.0
0.80	37.5
1.00	50.0
1.25	62.5
1.40	70.0

(i) Draw a graph of these results on the grid. The scale for the x-axis has been done for you.

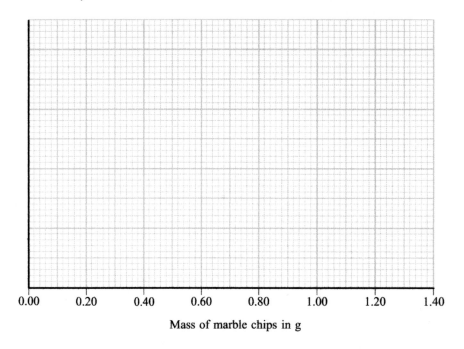

Mass of marble chips in g

[4]

(ii) Describe how the rate of the reaction increases as the mass of marble chips changes.

_____

_____ [2]

(iii) Give an explanation for this change in rate as the mass of marble chips increases.

_____

_____

_____

_____ [2]

(d) Suggest a different way in which the original experiment could be improved to make it a fair test.

_____

_____ [1]

[Total 14 marks]

More questions on the CD ROM

I (a) Ammonia is made industrially by the Haber process. In this process nitrogen is reacted with hydrogen. The flow diagram shows what happens in the Haber process.

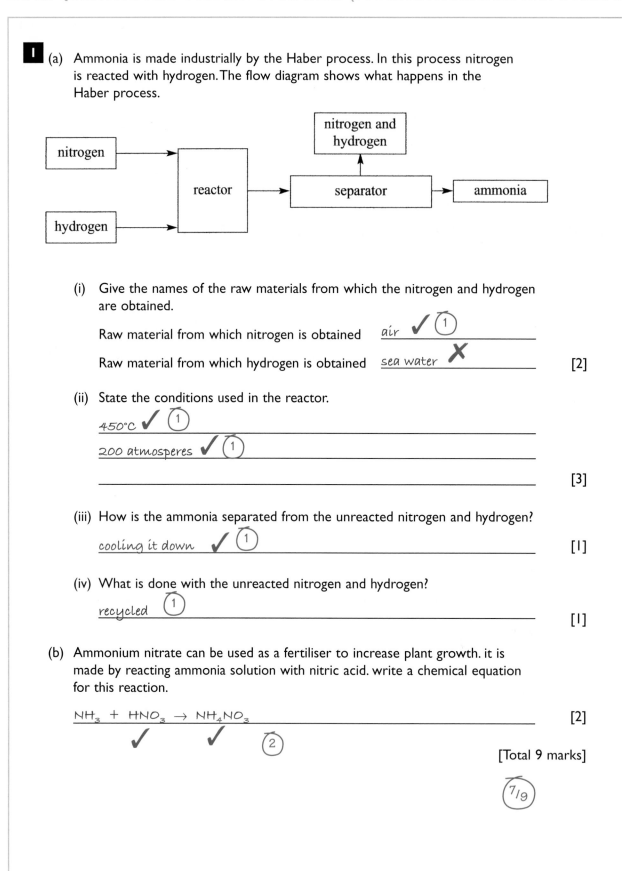

    (i) Give the names of the raw materials from which the nitrogen and hydrogen are obtained.

        Raw material from which nitrogen is obtained   air ✔ ①

        Raw material from which hydrogen is obtained   sea water ✘   [2]

    (ii) State the conditions used in the reactor.

        450°C ✔ ①

        200 atmosperes ✔ ①

         [3]

    (iii) How is the ammonia separated from the unreacted nitrogen and hydrogen?

        cooling it down ✔ ①   [1]

    (iv) What is done with the unreacted nitrogen and hydrogen?

        recycled ①   [1]

(b) Ammonium nitrate can be used as a fertiliser to increase plant growth. it is made by reacting ammonia solution with nitric acid. write a chemical equation for this reaction.

    $NH_3 + HNO_3 \rightarrow NH_4NO_3$ [2]

        ✔   ✔ ②

         [Total 9 marks]

         ⑦/₉

HOW TO SCORE FULL MARKS

a) i) Correct response.

ii) The hydrogen is obtained from oil or natural gas (methane is not acceptable as an answer).

b) The two answers given are correct BUT iron (catalyst) is the missing third mark. The candidate may well have known this but did not recognise it as a 'condition' for the reaction.

c) Correct response – 'condensed' or 'liquified' are equally acceptable.

d) Correct – this is an equilibrium process so some will be re-used.

e) Correct – 1 mark for correct formulae of reactants and 1 mark for correct product(s) formulae.

Also correct: $NH_4OH + HNO_3 \rightarrow NH_4NO_3 + H_2O$

QUESTION TO TRY (FOUNDATION/HIGHER TIER OVERLAP)

I This question is about the synthetic polymer nylon.

(a) Ploy(ethene) is an addition polymer. What type of polymer is nylon?

_____ [1]

(b) Nylon can be made using the monomers A and B represented in the diagrams.

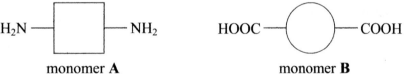

monomer **A**   monomer **B**

(i) What type of compound is monomer A?

_____ [1]

(ii) What type of compound is monomer B?

_____ [1]

(iii) Draw a diagram to show the structure of the polymer formed from A and B. You must draw enough of the structure to make the repeat unit clear.

[3]

(c) Nylon has a simple molecular structure. Use words from the box to complete the sentences.

Each word may be used once, more than once or not at all.

ions	high	low
molecules	strong	weak

Nylon has a _____ melting point. This is because there are _____

forces between the _____ that make up the structure. [3]

[Total 9 marks]

1 Diamond and graphite are different forms of carbon.

(a) State the term used to describe different forms of the same element in the same physical state.

allotropes ✔ ① [1]

(b) Name and describe the type of bonding in diamond.

Diamond is a giant structure where every carbon atom is joined to

four other carbon atoms in a tetrahedral shape ✗ [3]

(c) State one industrial use of diamond.

drilling ✔ ① [1]

(d) Graphite has a hexagonal layer structure. Draw a diagram, showing three hexagons, to show the atoms and bonding in graphite.

✔

✔

[2]

(e) Diamond and graphite both have high sublimation points. Explain why.

Both are giant structures with lots of strong bonds ✔ _holding them_

together. It takes a lot of heat energy ✔ _to break them up._ [2]

[Total 9 marks]

⑥⁄₉

HOW TO SCORE FULL MARKS

a) Correct response.

b) The candidate has given a correct description of the structure of diamond but has not answered the question about the **bonding**.

The correct response would mention covalent bonds (1) which are a shared pair of electrons (1), and the attraction between the nuclei and the bond pairs (1).

c) Correct response – grinding or cutting are also correct.

d) Answers the question asked about 3 rings and showing all carbon atoms.

e) Correct response which again answers the question asked.

QUESTION TO TRY (HIGHER TIER)

I The diagram shows the apparatus used to electrolyse lead(II) bromide.

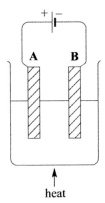

heat

(a) The wires connected to the electrodes are made of copper.

Explain why copper conducts electricity.

_____

_____ [1]

(b) Explain why electrolysis does not occur unless the lead(II) bromide is molten.

_____

_____ [2]

(c) The reactions occurring at the electrodes can be represented by the equations shown in the table.

Complete the table to show the electrode (A or B) at which each reaction occurs, and the type of reaction occurring (oxidation or reduction).

Electrode reaction	Electrode	Type of reaction
$Pb^{2+} + 2e^- \rightarrow Pb$		
$2Br^- \rightarrow Br_2 + 2e^-$		

[2]

(d) In an experiment using the same apparatus, the amount of charge passed was 0.10 faraday.

(i) Calculate the maximum amount in moles, of each substance formed.

Amount of Pb. _____

Amount of Br_2 _____ [2]

(ii) calculate the mass of bromine formed.

_____

_____ [2]

More questions
on the CD ROM

[Total 9 marks]

Foundation Tier (page 152)

Q1 a

metals	(1)
non-metals (either order)	(1)
gained	(1)
lost	(1)
high	(1)
high	(1)

This question relies on a basic understanding of the two types of bonding, i.e. ionic and covalent, and the properties of the compounds formed.

Although this question only asks about ionic it is important to think about both types so the words metal/non-metal and low/high are used correctly in the passage.

b (i) 2,8,2 (Mg) and 2,8,7 (Cl) either way round (1)(1)

Metals have electrons to gain noble gas configurations and non-metals gain electrons. Mg and Cl can be found in the periodic table for their configurations ((b)(i)) and losing/gaining gives the noble gas configurations ((b)(ii)).

(ii) 2,8 (Mg^{2+}) and 2,8,8 (Cl^-) (1)(1)

Alternative to coursework (pages 155–157)

Q1 a Gas syringe, drawn horizontally, to collect gas.

This is the usual way of collecting gases. 'A graduated tube over a bowl of water' should not be used because some gases are soluble in water and carbon dioxide is one of these gases.

b Table has:

Columns for: volume (gas), mass (solid), tile (1)

Units for all 3 columns (1)

All data included in table (1)

Being able to record data from experiments is an important skill. Often it is 'units that are omitted.

c (i) Correct scale for y-axis (1 cm = 10 cm^3) and labelled 'volume of gas cm^3' (1)

Correct plot of 6/7 points (2)

(4 or 5 points = 1 mark only).

Straight line of best fit (going though 0, 0) (1)

Omitting units on graphs costs marks as does not going through 0, 0 (origin) with a straight line of best fit.

(ii) As mass increases, rate increases (1)

directly proportional/double one, double the other (2)

N.B. Mark for first statement only if second statement incorrect Total (2)

The more precise statement about proportionality is worth the max. 2 marks, while the first statement is correct but does not state the relationship that is shown be the results.

(iii) The bigger mass has a bigger surface area (1) doubling the mass doubles the surface area/more frequent collisions. (1)

The two marks allocated should be a 'clue' that two pertinent statements need to be made.

d Collect the same volume of gas (and measure the time taken).

The ability to identify 'fairness' is important in experimental skills. it is about keeping some variables fixed and measuring others that change.

Foundation/Higher Tier overlap (pages 159–160)

Q1 a Condensation (1)

There are two types of polymerisation, 'condensation' (two different reacting molecules) and 'addition' (identical molecules with double carbon bonds).

b i) (di)amine – accept 'amino' (1)

ii) (di)carboxylic acid (1)

iii)

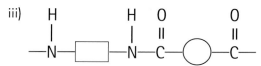

(1) alternating circle/square

(1) correct -NH-CO-

(1) continuation bonds at either end

Total (3)

Nylon is specifically stated in the syllabus as condensation polymerisation. It needs to be learnt thoroughly, i.e. the reacting molecules ((b)(i) + (ii)) and the polymer ((b)(iii)). Notice that the polymer needs to be shown 'continuing on' by the bonds at each end.

c   low (1)

   weak (1)

   molecules (1)

   The structure and properties of nylon need to be remembered. The question should 'clue you in' by giving the words to choose from.

Higher Tier (pages 162–163)

Q1 a   Electrons free to move/flow/mobile (1)

   Metals conduct electricity because of the delocalised electrons that are free to move ('sea of electrons' theory).

b   ions (1) cannot move unless molten (or in solution)/fixed positions in solids (1)

   This is the basic concept in electrolysis of ionic compounds. Notice the question does not mention that lead (II) bromide is ionic which is why 'ions' gains a mark in the answer.

c   B or (-) reduction (both) (1)

   A or (+) oxidation (both) (1)

   B and A can be identified as the cathode and the anode from the diagram or from the ions attracted to them in the table. Oxidation/reduction come from the definitions of loss or gain of electrons by the ions.

d   (i) Pb 0.05 moles (1)

       Br_2 0.05 moles (1)

   (ii) M_r of Br_2 = 160 (1)

   mass = 160 x 0.05 = 8 g (1)

   The calculation is based on 1 faraday being related to 1 mole of electrons.

   Pb^{2+} needs 2F for 1 mole, as does Br_2 (or 2 x Br^-) so 0.1 F → 0.05 moles. The mass of bromine is a conversion from moles to grams.

Answers and Solutions

1 PRINCIPLES OF CHEMISTRY

Atoms

Q1 Matter is made of tiny, indivisible particles which are in constant motion in gases and liquids.

Q2 Diffusion is the movement of gas or liquid particles from one place to another.

Q3 Ammonia will diffuse faster because it has the smaller molecule.

Atomic structure

Q1 a 2 moles

Moles = mass/Ar = 56/28 = 2

b 0.1 mole

Moles = mass/Ar = 3.1/31 = 0.1

Q2 a The atomic number is the number of protons in an atom. (It is equal to the number of electrons.)

Always define atomic number in terms of protons. However, as atoms are neutral there will always be equal numbers of protons and electrons.

b The mass number is the total number of protons and neutrons in an atom.

Remember that electrons have very little mass and so mass number cannot refer to electrons.

Q3

Si	14	14	14	2,8,4
Mg	12	14	12	2,8,2
S	16	16	16	2,8,6
Ar	18	22	18	2,8,8

The top number is the mass number and the bottom (smaller) number is the atomic number. The difference between the two numbers is the number of neutrons.

Q4 a (i) C; (ii) B; (iii) C or E or F; (iv) B; (v) C

To have no overall charge the number of protons (positive charges) must equal the number of electrons (negative charges). The atomic number (number of protons) is unique to a particular element. It is the atomic number that defines the element's position in the periodic table.

b 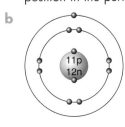 Remember that an atomic diagram should show the number of protons and neutrons in the nucleus and the number and arrangement of electrons.

(diagram label: 11p 12n)

Relative formula masses and molar volumes

Q1 a 0.25

b 0.1

c 3

Q2 a 220 g

b 10 g

c 10.9 g

Q3 a 560 tonnes

Fe_2O_3 = 1 mole → 160 tonnes. 2Fe = 2 moles → 112 tonnes.

b 144 litres at room temperature and pressure

Fe_2O_3 = 1 mole → 160 g. $3CO_2$ = 3 × 24 = 72 litres.

Chemical formulae and chemical equations

Q1 a $C + O_2 \rightarrow CO_2$

This doesn't need balancing!

b $4Fe + 3O_2 \rightarrow 2Fe_2O_3$

Remember that balancing numbers must always go in front of symbols and formulae.

c $2Fe_2O_3 + 3C \rightarrow 4Fe + 3CO_2$

One maths trick to use here is to realise that the number of oxygen atoms on the right-hand side must be even. Putting a '2' in front of Fe_2O_3 makes the oxygen on the left-hand side even too.

d $CaCO_3 + 2HCl \rightarrow CaCl_2 + CO_2 + H2O$

Note that the carbonate radical does not appear on both sides of the equation.

Q2 a $Ca^{2+} + CO_3^{2-} \rightarrow CaCO_3$

b $Fe^{2+} + 2OH^- \rightarrow Fe(OH)_2$

c $Ag^+ + Br^- \rightarrow AgBr$

The symbols and charges must balance on each side of the equation. State symbols could be used,

e.g. $Fe^{2+}(aq) + 2OH^-(aq) \rightarrow Fe(OH)_2(s)$

$Ag^+(aq) + Br^-(aq) \rightarrow AgBr(s)$.

Q3 4 g

2Na = 2 moles = 46 g. 2NaOH = 2 moles = 80 g.

Q4 Moles barium chloride = 50/1000 × 0.2
= 0.01
Moles barium sulphate = 0.01
Mass = 0.01 x 233 = 2.33 gms

Q5 $TiCl_4$

	Ti	Cl
mass/RAM	25/48	75/35.5
moles	0.52	2.1
ratio	0.52/0.52 = 1	2.1/0.52 = 4.04

formula is $TiCl_4$

Q6 **a** NaBr

0.1 mol Na reacts with 0.1 mol Br,
i.e. ratio 1:1.

b CO_2

0.05 mol C reacts with 1.6/16 = 0.10 mol
O, i.e. ratio 1:2.

c $FeCl_3$

0.2 mol Fe reacts with 0.6 mol Cl,
i.e. ratio 1:3.

Ionic compounds

Q1 **a** Covalent

b covalent

c ionic

d covalent

e ionic.

Remember that ionic bonding involves a metal
and a non-metal; covalent bonding involves two
or more non-metals. Hydrogen, chlorine, carbon,
oxygen and bromine are non-metals.
Only sodium and calcium in the list are metals.

Q2 **a** K^+

b Al^{3+}

c S^{2-}

d F^-

These can be worked out from the position of the
element in the periodic table. Look back in the
unit for the rule if you have forgotten it. You will
always be given a periodic table in the exam.
Get used to using it: it will help you to gain
marks in the exam.

Q3 **a** Potassium chloride exists as a giant ionic
lattice. There are very strong electrostatic
forces holding the ions together. A
considerable amount of energy is needed
to overcome the forces of attraction so the
melting point is high.

The key ideas relating to melting point are:
strong forces between particles; large
amounts of energy needed to overcome
these forces.

b Potassium chloride is ionically bonded.
When molten or dissolved in water the
ions are free to move and carry an electric
current.

Remember that an electrolyte allows an
electric current to flow through it when
molten or dissolved in water – not when in
the solid state.

Covalent substances

Q1 **a**

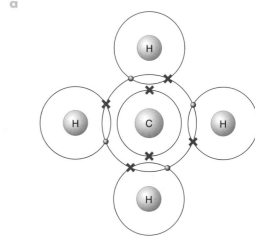

b

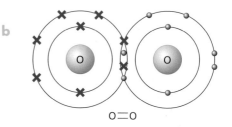

O=O

c

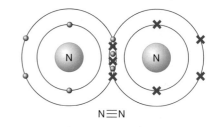

N≡N

d

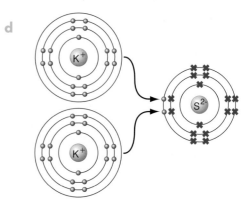

e

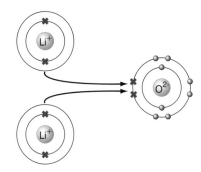

1 Remember that covalent compounds contain non-metals.

2 You can get the atomic number (needed to work out the number of electrons) from the periodic table.

3 With covalent compounds try drawing the displayed formula first. You will need to work out how many covalent bonds each atom can form. Again, the periodic table will help you. For example, oxygen is in Group 6 so it can form two covalent bonds. Once you have got the displayed formula, each bond corresponds to a shared pair of electrons. Don't forget the first electron shell can hold 2 electrons, others hold 8 electrons. So don't miss any electrons out.

4 In examples of ionic bonding don't forget to write the formulae of the ions that are formed.

Q2 a The carbon atoms are held by strong covalent bonds within the hexagonal layers. This can give a structure great strength.

Have a look at the diagram of the structure of graphite. Remember that covalent bonds are strong bonds.

b Only three out of the four of carbon's outer shell electrons are used in forming covalent bonds. Each atom has an electron which is only loosely held to the atom. When a voltage is applied these electrons move, forming an electric current.

Graphite has a structure similar to that of metals – there is a 'cloud' of electrons which are free to move.

Q3 The bonds within the molecule are strong (the intramolecular bonds) but the bonds holding the methane molecules together are weak (intermolecular bonds). Therefore methane molecules require very little energy to be separated from each other.

This is one of the ideas candidates find very confusing. Always try to be precise. There are bonds within a molecule as well as bonds between molecules. You wouldn't be expected to use 'intramolecular' and 'intermolecular', but if you do be sure to get them the right way round!

Electrolysis

Q1 a This is the breakdown (decomposition) of a compound using electricity.

If you are still puzzled by electrolysis look back at page 40.

b This is a substance which when molten or dissolved in water allows an electric current to pass through it and is broken down by it.

Electrolytes must contain ions and the ions must be free to move before a current will flow.

c This is the substance which makes the electrical contact between the battery and the electrolyte.

In a circuit there will always be two electrodes.

d This is the electrode connected to the positive terminal of the battery.

Ions that travel to the anode are called anions (negatively charged ions).

e This is the electrode connected to the negative terminal of the battery.

Ions that travel to the cathode are called cations (positively charged ions)

Q2 a $Al^{3+} + 3e^- \rightarrow Al$

b $Na \rightarrow Na^+ + e^-$

c $2O^{2-} \rightarrow O_2 + 4e^-$

d $2Br^- \rightarrow Br_2 + 2e^-$

At the cathode positive ions gain electrons. At the anode negative ions lose electrons. Remember that symbols and charges must balance.

Q3 Solid ZnBr does not conduct because ions cannot move.

Q4 a cathode: sodium; anode: chlorine

b cathode: hydrogen; anode: chlorine

Q5 cathode: the fork; anode: pure silver

Q6 $Ag^+ + e^- \rightarrow Ag$

$2I^- + 2e^- \rightarrow I_2$

Metallic crystals

Q1 In graphite, electrons can only move along the layers of atoms (in one plane) but not between them. In metals, the electrons can move in any plane as the lattice is symmetrical in all directions.

This is the fundamental difference between the conduction of electricity in metals and graphite. Both contain delocalised electrons, but graphite electrons can only move along the layers and not between them.

Q2 a C is a metal.

Conducts as solid and liquid.

b A contains ionic bonds.

Conducts when molten but not as solid.

c D has a giant covalent structure.

Does not conduct electricity but has high melting and boiling points.

d B has a simple molecular structure.

Does not conduct electricity but has low melting and boiling points.

2 CHEMISTRY OF THE ELEMENTS
The Periodic table

Q1 a b

Group 4 is the fourth major column from the left.

b a

This is the second row.

c d

The noble gas family is group 0 or 8.

d c

Transition elements are in the middle block.

e d and f

These are on the right of the periodic table. If you included b you would not be penalised.

f d

Gases are non-metals and so have to be on the right side. f is a possibility but in groups 5, 6 and 7 elements near the bottom of the group are solids.

Q2 They contain the same number of electrons in the outer electron shell.

Remember that how an atom reacts depends on its outermost electrons.

Q3 a Down a metallic group the elements become more reactive and reactivity increases.

b Down a non-metallic group the elements become less reactive and reactivity decreases.

Q4 Metals lose electrons, non-metals gain electrons.

Q5 large metal atoms are more reactive than smaller ones in the same group because they lose electrons more easily, there is more shielding of the nucleus by electron levels and there are more electron levels.

The Group 1 elements - lithium, sodium and potassium

Q1 a Caesium.

Remember that the reactivity of metals increases down a group.

b To prevent the metal reacting with air and water.

These are highly reactive metals. They oxidise rapidly without heat being needed.

c Caesium.

The melting point gives a measure of hardness. Melting point decreases down the group.

d On cutting, the metal is exposed to the air and rapidly oxidises.

Tarnishing is another word for oxidation.

e When added to water they react to produce an alkali.

The metal hydroxides formed in the reactions are alkalis.

f Sodium is less dense than water.

Density increases down the group. The more reactive metals would not float but their reaction is so violent that the metal usually flies out of the water!

Q2 a (i) rubidium + oxygen → rubidium oxide

$4Rb(s) + O_2(g) \rightarrow 2Rb_2O(s)$

Rubidium behaves in the same way as sodium but more violently.

b (ii) caesium + water → caesium hydroxide + hydrogen

$2Cs(s) + 2H_2O(l) \rightarrow 2CsOH(aq) + H_2(g)$

The reaction of the group 1 metals with water produces the metal hydroxide (an alkali) and hydrogen.

c (iii) potassium + chlorine → potassium chloride

$2K(s) + Cl_2(g) \rightarrow 2KCl(s)$

Potassium chloride is a salt with an appearance very similar to sodium chloride, common salt.

Q3 a In bonding, lithium loses an electron to form a positive ion (cation).

b Lithium is the smallest atom and has fewest electron levels to shield its outer electron from the pull of the nucleus. The outer electron is closest to the nucleus.

Q4 They would react with water vapour in the air.

Q5 a $4K(s) + O_2(g) \rightarrow 2K_2O(s)$

b $2Na(s) + 2H_2O(l) \rightarrow 2NaOH(aq) + H_2(g)$

The Group 2 elements – magnesium and calcium

Q1 **a** Of magnesium and calcium, calcium is the more reactive.

b Magnesium is the least reactive of the two.

c Metals become more reactive as the atoms become larger.

d The metals are harder and with a higher melting point than Group 1 metals because they can share two electrons into the metal structure. The metal ions are more highly charged and hold the lattice together more strongly.

e **i** $Mg + O_2 \rightarrow MgO$

ii $Ca + 2H_2O \rightarrow Ca(OH)_2 + H_2$

iii $Sr + 2F_2 \rightarrow SrF_2$

Q2 Reactivity increases.

Q3 Group 2 metals have to lose 2 electrons in bonding to gain the configurations of noble gases. Group 1 metals only have to lose 1 electron which requires less energy.

The group 7 elements - chlorine, bromine and iodine

Q1 **a** Fluorine

Unlike groups of metals, reactivity decreases down the group.

b Bromine

Bromine is the only liquid non-metal.

c Iodine

Astatine would be expected to be a solid but it is radioactive with a very short half-life so it is difficult to confirm this prediction.

d They only need to gain one electron in order to have a full outer electron shell. Other non-metals need to gain more than one electron.

Remember that reactivity depends on the number of electrons in the outer electron shell.

Q2 **a** sodium + chlorine → sodium chloride

$2Na(s) + Cl_2(g) \rightarrow 2NaCl(s)$

b magnesium + bromine → magnesium bromide

$Mg(s) + Br_2(l) \rightarrow MgBr_2(s)$

c hydrogen + fluorine → hydrogen fluoride

$H_2(g) + F_2(g) \rightarrow 2HF(g)$

Q3 Bromine + sodium iodide → iodine + sodium bromide

$Br_2(aq) + 2NaI(aq) \rightarrow I_2(aq) + 2NaBr(aq)$

Bromine is more reactive than iodine and so will displace it from the solution. In this reaction it would be difficult to see a change as both the bromine and iodine solutions are brown. Using cyclohexane would confirm that a reaction had taken place.

Q4 Group 7 element are non-metallic, so in bonding they need to gain electrons to form negative ions (anions). As you go up from group 7 the atoms become smaller so there is less shielding of the pull of the nucleus by the fewer electron orbits. This makes it easier for the smaller atoms to attract electrons.

Oxygen and oxides

Q1 Oxygen is obtained from liquid air by fractional distillation.

Q2 Iron rusts when it reacts with oxygen in the air and water on the surface of the iron.

Q3 **a** When iron is coated with a layer of zinc this is called galvanising.

b Zinc protects the iron from rusting because it reacts first in preference to the iron. This is called sacrificial protection.

Q4 $Na_2O(s) + H_2O(l) \rightarrow 2NaOH(aq)$

Sulphur

Q1 Bleach in paper production, and as a food preservative (to kill bacteria).

Q2 Add dilute acid and test for the production of sulphur dioxide gas using potassium dichromate paper (goes from yellow to green).

Nitrogen and ammonia

Q1 The fractional distillation of liquid air.

Q2 **a** It is not very reactive

b Any suitable e.g. making ammonia, liquid nitrogen for freezing, creating an inert atmosphere for preserving food or preventing oxidation in some processes

c Two atoms in the molecule (N_2)

Q3 Add dilute sodium hydroxide solution and warm. Test any gas give off with damp red litmus paper. If the paper goes blue then ammonia has been given off, showing the presence of ammonium ions.

Hydrogen

Q1 "Pops/squeaks' with a lighted splint.

Q2 $2H_2(g) + O_2(g) \rightarrow 2H_2O(l)$

Q3 Advantage – only produces water on combustion so better for the environment.

Disadvantage – dangerous, tank could explode if car involved in collision.

The transition metals – iron and copper

Q1 **a** $2Fe(s) + 3Cl_2(g) \rightarrow 2FeCl_3(s)$

b $Fe(s) + 2HCl(g) \rightarrow FeCl_2(s) + H_2(g)$

Q2 **a** A green precipitate (of $Fe(OH)_2$)

b The green precipitate goes brown (oxidised to $Fe(OH)_3$)

Q3 Electrical cables and cooking utensils.

Reactivity series

Q1 **a** $CuO + H_2 \rightarrow Cu + H_2O$

b Hydrogen is more reactive than copper

Q2 **a** Displacement

b Zinc is more reactive than copper

Q3 React one metal with the oxide of another metal. If there is a reaction, the metal is more reactive than the metal in the oxide (a displacement reaction).

Q4 **a** Sacrificial protection

b Zinc is more reactive than iron so corrodes instead of the iron.

Preparing and analysing

Q1 'Corrosive' means it can damage the skin, so gloves should be worn when handling it. Because it is 'highly flammable' it gives off vapours (evaporates easily) so it should be used in a fume cupboard so that it does not catch fire.

You cannot give the safety precautions needed without explaining the specific effects indicated by the hazard symbols.

Q2 Put a piece of damp blue litmus paper which will go first red (it is acidic), then white (it is a bleach).

Q3 Perform a flame test. If a lilac/purple flame is seen it shows the presence of potassium ions. Add dilute acid to the solid and pass any gases through limewater. If the limewater goes cloudy/milky then carbon dioxide has been produced from a carbonate in the solid.

Q4 **a** Dissolve the compound in water, add dilute hydrochloric acid and then barium chloride solution. A white precipitate shows the presence of a sulphate ion.

b Dissolve the compound in water, add dilute nitric acid followed by silver nitrate solution. A yellow precipitate shows the presence of the iodide ion.

ATION AND SOLUTIONS

3 ORGANIC CHEMISTRY

Alkanes

Q1 **a** Members of the same family which differ by one carbon atom each time, i.e. $-CH_2-$ is added.

b Molecules with the same number and type of atoms but arranged in different ways.

Q2 **a** Two isomers of butane:

and

Alkenes

Q1 **a** (i)

hexane

(ii) hexene

Remember 'hex' means 6. The ending 'ane' means only single bonds whereas 'ene' means there is a carbon–carbon double bond.

b Add bromine water. It will be decolourised by hexene but not by hexane.

This is the standard test for all alkenes. You should give the test reagent and what you would observe.

Q2 Two isomers of butene:

and

It is always easiest to draw the long straight-chain isomer, then to take a –CH3 off one end and put it somewhere else in the, now shorter, chain. Don't forget to count the C's and H's to make sure they add up to the original formula.

Ethanol

Q1 **a** Yeast contains an enzyme that converts sugar to ethanol. Enzymes work at a low optimum temperature. If the temperature rises above 30 °C, the enzyme is denatured and the reaction stops.

This topic involves work on enzymes from Unit 9, and the basic facts about these biological catalysts is an integral part of the work on fermentation.

b Oxygen from the air would oxidise the ethanol to ethanoic acid ('vinegar'). This is 'spoilage'.

As an oxidation process, changing alcohols to carboxylic acids, is a fundamental part of the chemistry syllabus.

Q2 Two isomers of butanol:

and

As with the isomers of hydrocarbons, the simplest way is the best in such questions. Start with the –OH group at the end of the longest straight carbon chain and then put it on another carbon atom in the chain.

Q3 The reaction between an alcohol and a carboxylic acid to form an ester.

This is a basic reaction of alcohols and carboxylic acids. Esters are vital components of perfumes.

173

4 PHYSICAL CHEMISTRY

What are the states of matter?

Q1 Gas

The particles are moving faster and are further apart.

Q2 The forces between atoms in the aluminium must be greater than those in sodium.

More energy is needed to separate the aluminium particles.

Q3 When steam condenses to water it gives out a lot of energy.

The steam contains the energy associated with a change of state.

Q4 There is no temperature change at a change of state because the energy is being used to separate the particles.

This is the fundamental point about changes of state.

Q5 Condensing

Gas to liquid is shown by the state symbols.

Acidity, alkalinity and neutralisation

Q1 **a** A substance that changes colour to show if a solution is acidic, neutral or alkaline (basic).

Litmus as red, purple or blue is linked to acidic; neutral and alkaline need to be remembered as conditions shown by an indicator.

b The numbers 1 to 14 linked to the strengths of acids and alkalis (bases).

pH 1 to 6 is strongly acidic to weakly acidic, pH 7 is neutral and pH 8 to 14 is weakly alkaline to strongly alkaline.

c Each colour from Universal Indicator has a pH number.

Remember pH 1-2 is maroon/red, pH 7 is yellow-green and pH 13-14 is blue/purple.

Q2 **a** An acid that totally dissociates into ions, so releasing all its available H+ ions.

This is 'strong' as opposed to 'weak' (partial dissociation).

b $H_3PO_4(aq) \rightarrow 3H^+(aq) + PO_4^{3-}(aq)$

For a strong acid you need to use the arrow symbol, $\rightarrow$. Phosphoric acid is tribasic, so producing 3 x H$^+$.

c pH = 1 to 2

Strong acids are in this range on the pH scale, and maroon/red as UI colours.

Q3 **a** Only partially dissociates into ions.

As opposed to 'strong' which is complete dissociation to ions.

b $HCOOH(aq) \rightleftharpoons HCOO^-(aq) + H^+(aq)$

Methanoic acid is monobasic (one H$^+$) and, since it is weak, there is an equilibrium shown by the $\rightleftharpoons$ sign.

Q4 **a** $K_2SO_4(aq) + 2H_2O(l)$

alkali + acid $\rightarrow$ soluble salt + water

b $MgCl_2(aq) + H_2O(l)$

acid + base $\rightarrow$ soluble salt + water

c $Ba(NO_3)_2(aq) + CO_2(g) + H_2O(l)$

acid + carbonate $\rightarrow$ soluble salt + carbon dioxide + water

d $ZnCl_2(aq) + H_2(g)$

acid + metal $\rightarrow$ soluble salt + hydrogen

e $ZnCO_3(s) + 2KCl(aq)$

soluble salt + soluble salt $\rightarrow$ insoluble salt + soluble salt

The issue is which of the two salts is insoluble. You need to remember that in this method it is usually sodium or potassium salts that are used as one of the reactants – sodium and potassium salts are almost always soluble.

Energetics

Q1 **a** Energy = $40 \times 4.2 \times 32 = 5376$ J.

b Energy = $5376/0.2 = 26\ 880$ J/g.

Use the formula energy = mass $\times$ 4.2 $\times$ temperature change.

Q2 **a** The reaction is exothermic.

b More energy is released when bonds are formed than is used to break the bonds in the first place.

In an energy level diagram, if the products are lower in energy than the reactants the reaction change is exothermic. Remember that the overall energy change = energy needed to break bonds – energy released on forming bonds.

Q3 More energy is released when the H—Cl bonds are made than is needed to break the H—H and Cl—Cl bonds. The overall energy change is therefore exothermic.

Again this refers to the balance between bond breaking and bond forming. Always refer to the specific bonds involved.

Q4 **a** Total bonds on left:

4 × C–H	4 × 413
2 × O=O	2 × 498
Total	+2648 kJ mol^{-1}

Total bonds on right:

2 × C=O	2 × 745	= 1490
4 × O–H	4 × 464	
Total	–3346 kJ mol^{-1}	
Overall:	–3346	
	+2648	
	–698	

Answer: ΔH = –698 kJ mol^{-1}

The bonds on the left of the equation are broken, so a + sign; those on the right are made, so a – sign.

b The – sign shows the reaction is exothermic.

In a question of this type, even if you make an error in the sign you will gain the mark for correctly liking it to exothermic or endothermic.

Rates of reaction

Q1 **a** Not all collisions provide enough energy for the reaction to take place.

Energy is needed to break chemical bonds so that the atoms, molecules or ions can rearrange and form new bonds. Remember that collisions that do have sufficient energy are referred to as effective collisions.

Q2 Reaction A.

Reaction A has a lower activation energy than reaction B. This means that there will be more effective collisions and so the rate of reaction will be higher. If you are still not clear about this idea of an 'energy barrier', look again at the explanation of activation energy in the collision theory section.

Q3 **a** Carbon dioxide

Remember that marble has the chemical name calcium carbonate. The carbon dioxide is released from the carbonate ion.

b (i) 20 cm^3; (ii) 16 cm^3; (iii) 13 cm^3; (iv) 0 cm^3.

20 – 0 = 20; 36 – 20 = 16; 49 – 36 = 13; 70 – 70 = 0. Don't forget the units of volume.

c The volume of gas produced in each 10 second interval decreases as the reaction proceeds. This means the rate of production of gas decreases.

The rate of reaction is measured in terms of the volume of gas produced in a certain amount of time. If you wanted to calculate rates in these time intervals you would need to divide the volume of gas produced by the time taken. So between 0 and 10 seconds 20 cm^3 of gas was collected giving a rate of 20/10 = 2 cm^3/s. Between 20 and 30 seconds the rate was 1.3 cm^3/s.

d As the reaction proceeds there are fewer particles of hydrochloric acid and calcium carbonate to collide with each other. Therefore there will be fewer collisions and hence fewer effective collisions.

Don't forget to mention the idea of 'effective collisions' (see page 89). This is a key idea in this chapter. If you want to impress the examiner use the correct names for the particles – e.g. in this reaction collisions occur between hydrogen ions (H+ ions) and carbonate ions (CO_3^{2-} ions).

e Measuring the change in mass as the reaction proceeds.

The carbon dioxide gas will escape, causing a decrease in mass of the reaction container. The equipment you would need is shown on page 91.

Q4 As the temperature increases, the kinetic energy of the reacting particles also increases. The particles will therefore be moving faster and will collide more frequently. In addition, there will be more energy transferred in the collisions and so more are likely to be effective and lead to a reaction.

Don't forget to mention the energy of the collision. Many students only mention the increased number of collisions.

Q5 **a** i) Experiment 1; (ii) the reaction finishes more quickly because the curve levels out soonest.

A better answer would mention the gradient of the curve – e.g. the gradient of the curve at the beginning of the reaction is the steepest.

b (i) Experiment 3; (ii) the largest chips have the smallest surface area and so the lowest rate of reaction.

The curve for experiment 3 has the lowest gradient at the beginning of the reaction. If you got this wrong check the section on surface area again.

c (i) 7.5 minutes (approximately); (ii) the reaction finished because the marble was used up.

Try to read off the graph as accurately as you can. In an examination you will be allowed a small margin of error. In this example 7.3 to 7.7 minutes would be acceptable. The question says that the hydrochloric acid was 'an excess'. This means that there was more than would be needed. Therefore the reaction must have finished because the marble was used up. Always look for the phrase 'an excess' or 'in excess'.

d The same mass of marble was used in each experiment.

As the acid is in excess the amount of marble will determine how much carbon dioxide is produced.

e The curve would be steeper (have a higher gradient) at the beginning of the reaction but would reach the same plateau height.

Increasing the temperature will increase the rate of the reaction but will not change the amount of carbon dioxide produced. If you are still in doubt about this read the section on temperature again.

Equilibria

Q1 A reaction is in equilibrium when the number of reactant and product molecules do not change.

You might remember that at equilibrium the rate of the forward reaction equals the rate of the backward reaction.

Q1 **a** It increases the rate.

b No affect on the yield.

5 CHEMISTRY IN SOCIETY
The extraction and uses of metals

Q1 **a** Iron oxide + carbon → iron + carbon dioxide

In the blast furnace much of the reduction is done by carbon monoxide.

b Reduced. Reduction is the loss of oxygen. The iron oxide has lost oxygen, forming iron.

Reduction and oxidation always occur together. In this reaction the carbon is oxidised.

c The limestone reacts with impurities, forming a slag that floats to the top and is removed from the furnace.

Of the three raw materials in the blast furnace (coke, iron ore, limestone) this is the easiest one to forget.

Q2 How reactive it is/its position in the reactivity series.

Q3 In their ores (compounds) the metals are cations. Adding electrons to cations to form ions is a reduction process.

Q4 The ions must be free to move. In a solid the ions are held in a giant lattice structure.

Remember that the ions in a solid can be made free to move by either melting the solid or dissolving it in water. Aluminium oxide does not dissolve in water.

Natural gas and oil

Q1 **a** Small sea creatures died, their bodies settled in the mud at the bottom of the oceans and decayed. They were compressed over a period of millions of years and slowly changed into crude oil.

Remember the process involves compression and takes place over millions of years. Do not confuse crude oil with coal, which is formed from plant material.

b It takes millions of years to form. Once supplies have been used up they cannot be replaced.

A common mistake is to say 'it cannot be used again'. No fuel can be used again but some, such as trees (wood), can be regrown quite quickly. Wood is therefore renewable.

Q2 a Fractional distillation.

There is often a mark for 'fractional' and a mark for 'distillation'.

b The boiling point of the fractions decreases.

Remember the column is hotter at the bottom than at the top.

c Components that have boiling points just above the temperature of X will condense to a liquid. Components which have boiling points below the temperature of X will remain as vapour and continue up the column.

If a vapour is cooled below its boiling point it will condense.

Q3 a A compound containing carbon and hydrogen atoms only.

Don't miss out the word 'only'. A lot of compounds contain carbon and hydrogen but are not hydrocarbons (e.g. glucose, $C_6H_{12}O_6$).

b High temperature, catalyst.

'Catalytic crackers' are used at oil refineries.

c C_8H_{18}.

The equation must balance so the number of carbon atoms must be 10 – 2, the number of hydrogen atoms 22 – 4.

Q4 A thin layer of oil spreads over large areas of the sea so preventing evaporation of water which would normally have gone into the atmosphere forming clouds.

Absence of clouds means absence of rainfall in some areas of the Earth.

Q5 a petrol + oxygen → carbon dioxide + water

All hydrocarbons produce carbon dioxide and water when burnt in a plentiful supply of air. It is much better to use oxygen rather than air in the equation.

b Shortage of oxygen.

Remember this is incomplete combustion.

c The carbon monoxide combines with the haemoglobin in the blood, preventing oxygen from doing so. Supply of oxygen to the body is reduced. Specifically this can quickly cause the death of brain cells.

A much more detailed answer is required than 'it causes suffocation'.

Synthetic polymers

Q1 a

b

c Poly(propene).

Just put 'poly' in front of the name of the monomer.

d Propane is saturated and doesn't have a carbon–carbon double bond to undergo addition reactions.

The carbon–carbon double bond is the reactive part of the molecule.

Q2 A monomer means there is one unit in the molecule. A polymer means several units have been joined together.

The manufacture of some important chemicals

Q1 The higher temperature is used to increase the rate of the reaction.

The choice of temperature in industrial processes often balances how much can be formed (depends on the equilibrium position) and how fast it can be formed (depends on the rate of the reaction).

Q2 The reaction:

$$SO_3(g) + H_2O(l) \rightarrow H_2SO_4(l)$$

is very exothermic. The heat makes the acid vaporise into a dangerous 'acid mist'.

To make sulphuric acid by way of 'oleum' seems unnecessary, until you recognise the exothermic nature of the reaction above.

Q3 a Burning fossil fuels that contain both sulphur and nitrogen. The oxides of sulphur and nitrogen react with water to form acids, e.g. sulphuric acid.

The key point is the presence of sulphur and nitrogen → SO_2 (and NO_2) and so to H_2SO_4.

b   Effect of sulphuric acid on buildings made of limestone/marble or metal. Effect on plants, leading to effect on animals. Leaching into rivers and lakes of aluminium which poisons fish.

There are many effects of acid rain and you need to focus on the key facts relating to the environment and hence animals/fish/plants.

Q4 a $Na^+ + e \rightarrow Na$

b $2Cl^- \rightarrow Cl_2 + 2e$

Q5 a   Cathode: $2H^+(aq) + 2e^- \rightarrow H_2(g)$

Anode: $2Cl^-(aq) \rightarrow Cl_2(g) + 2e^-$

These two elements are diatomic gaseous molecules.

b   Removal of H^+ and Cl^- from the solution leaves Na^+ and OH^-, i.e. $NaOH(aq)$.

It is important to remember there are four ions in sodium chloride solution.

Q6 'Chlor' comes from chlorine gas, and 'alkali' from sodium hydroxide.

Because only two products are mentioned in the term, do not forget there are three products of the process, i.e. hydrogen as well.

Q7 The chlorine and sodium hydroxide would react together to make NaOCl.

The fact that they react is the basic idea; quoting the product of the reaction is the fuller answer.

Q8 a   Chlorine bleaches damp litmus paper. It is used to kill bacteria in drinking water.

b   Hydrogen 'pops' with a lighted splint. It is used to make margarine.

The tests and uses need to be learned thoroughly.

GLOSSARY

Oil refinery, Malaysia

Potash mining, Canada

Singaporean silver coin

Diamonds are allotropes

Nebula gases

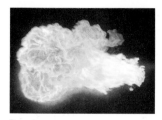

Burning

acid Substance with a pH less than 7. Acid molecules in solution release hydrogen ions, H^+.

activation energy The energy to be overcome before a reaction can take place.

alcohol Molecule with an –OH group attached to a chain of carbon atoms.

alkali Soluble substance with a pH greater than 7. Alkalis usually release hydroxide ions, OH^-.

alkali metal A Group 1 element.

alkane Hydrocarbon where the carbon atoms are bonded together by single bonds only.

alkene Hydrocarbon that contains a carbon-carbon double bond.

allotrope The different physical forms in which a pure element can exist.

anhydrous Literally means 'without water' – a compound with no water of crystallisation.

anode A positively charged electrode in electrolysis.

atom The smallest particle of an element. Atoms are made of protons, electrons and neutrons.

atomic number Number of protons in an atom.

Avogadro's constant The number of particles in one mole of a substance. It is 6.0×10^{23}

base Substance that neutralises an acid to produce a salt and water.

battery A series of cells connected together so as to provide an electric current.

boiling point The temperature of a boiling liquid – the highest temperature that the liquid can reach and the lowest temperature that the gas can reach.

burning The reaction of a substance with oxygen in a flame.

catalyst A chemical that is added to speed up a reaction, but remains unchanged at the end.

cathode A negatively charged electrode in electrolysis.

cell, chemical A device for turning chemical energy into electrical energy.

chemical change A change that is not easily reversed because new substances are made.

combustion The burning of a fuel in oxygen, also in air.

concentration Amount of chemical dissolved in 1 dm^3 of solvent.

covalent bond Bonding between atoms that depends on the sharing of a pair of electrons.

cracking Forming shorter alkanes and alkanes from longer alkanes using high temperatures and pressures.

decomposition Chemical change that breaks down one substance into two or more.

electrode The carbon or metal material that is given an electrical charge in electrolysis reactions.

electrolysis This involves breaking down a compound containing ions by the passage of an electric current. The compound must either be melted or dissolved in water.

electron Negatively charged particles with a negligible mass that form the outer portion of all atoms.

element A substance that cannot be broken down into other substances by any chemical change.

endothermic Type of reaction in which energy is transferred in from the surroundings.

enzyme Chemical that speeds up certain reactions in biological systems, e.g. digestive enzymes speed up the chemical digestion of food.

equilibrium reaction Chemical reaction where the forward and backward reactions are both likely, shown as: X ⇌ Y.

evaporation Liquid changes to gas at a temperature lower than the boiling point.

exothermic Type of reaction in which energy is transferred out to the surroundings.

fermentation Chemical decomposition by micro-organisms, e.g. yeast.

filtrate The clear solution produced by filtering a mixture.

formula mass (M_r) The sum of the atomic masses of the atoms in a formula.

fossil fuel Fuel made from the remains of decayed animal and plant matter compressed over millions of years.

fraction A collection of hydrocarbons that have similar molecular masses and boil at similar temperatures.

fractional distillation Separating fractions of a mixture by distilling. The process depends on the differences in boiling points of the fractions.

freezing Changing a liquid to a solid at the melting point.

group A vertical column of elements in the Periodic Table.

halogens Group 7 elements (F, Cl, Br, I, At). They have one electron missing from their outer shell.

Copper oxidation

Chemical change; nylon

Fireworks, China

Environmental pollution

Gold leaf

Waterfall, Thailand

Saudi Arabia, refinery

Dried fish, Thailand

Indian lattice pattern

Molten lead

Neon lights, Hong Kong

Norwegian oil platform

homologous series Molecules with the same functional group but with different lengths of carbon chain.

hydrated Literally means 'containing water' – hydrated salts contain water of crystallisation.

ion A charged atom or molecule.

ionic bonding Bonding that involves the transfer of electrons to produce electrically charged ions.

isomer A compound having the same molecular formula but different structures.

isotope Atoms of the same element that contain different numbers of neutrons. Isotopes have the same atomic number but different mass numbers.

melting Changing a solid into a liquid at the melting point.

mole An amount equal to the number of atoms in 12g of ^{12}C.

molecule A group of two or more atoms covalently bonded together.

monomer A small molecule that can be joined in a chain to make a polymer.

neutron Particle present in the nucleus of atoms that have mass but no charge.

noble gas Group O elements (He, Ne, Ar, Kr, Xe, Rn). They have full outer electron shells.

non-renewable Fuel that cannot be made again in a short time span.

nucleus, atomic The tiny centre of an atom made from protons and neutrons.

ore A mineral from which a metal may be extracted.

organic chemistry The study of covalent compounds of carbon.

organic molecules Carbon based molecules.

oxidation This happens when a substance gains oxygen in a chemical reaction. Oxidation is the loss of electrons.

percentage yield Fraction of substance produced (actual yield) in a chemical process compared to the possible predicted yield.

period Row in the Periodic Table, from an alkali metal to a noble gas.

pH scale Measure of the acidity (lower than 7) or alkalinity of a solution (greater than 7). It is a measure of the concentration of hydrogen ions in a solution.

photosynthesis A reaction that plants carry out to make food.

physical change A change in chemicals that is easily reversed and does not involve the making of new chemical bonds.

polymer Large molecule made up from smaller molecules. Polythene is a polymer made from ethene.

polymerisation Making polymers from monomers.

precipitation The formation of an insoluble solid when two solutions react together.

products The chemicals that are produced in a reaction.

proton Positively charged, massive particles found in the nucleus of an atom.

rate of reaction How fast a reaction goes in a given interval of time.

reactant The chemicals taking part in a chemical reaction. They change into the products.

reactivity series A list of elements showing their relative reactivity. More reactive elements will displace less reactive ones from their compounds.

reduction When a chemical loses oxygen. Reduction is the gain of electrons.

Relative Atomic Mass (A$_r$) A number comparing the mass of one mole of atoms of a particular element with the mass of one mole of atoms of other elements. C has the value12.

Relative Formula Mass (M$_r$) The sum of the relative atomic masses of each of the atoms in one mole of a substance.

reversible Describes a reaction that can go backwards as well as forwards.

salt Compound made from the reaction of an acid and a base.

saturated Describes an organic compound that contains only single bonds.

shell A grouping of electrons around a nucleus. The first shell in an atom can hold up to 2 electrons, the next two shells can hold up to 8 each.

solution This is formed when a substance dissolves into a liquid. Aqueous solutions are formed when the solvent used is water.

solvent The liquid in which solutes are dissolved.

speed of reaction How fast a reaction goes in a given interval of time.

state symbols These denote whether a substance is a solid (s), liquid (l), gas (g) or is dissolved in aqueous solution (aq).

surface area The total area of the outside of an object. Particles of chemical reactants can bombard only the surface of an object.

transition metal Elements found between Group 2 and 3 in the Periodic Table. Often used as catalysts and often make compounds that have coloured solutions.

universal indicator Indicating solution that turns a specific colour at each pH value.

unsaturated Describes carbon compounds that contain double bonds.

volatile Easily turning to a gas.

yield Amount of substance produced from a chemical reaction.

Grass, Bali

Polymer container

Bridge repainting

Space shuttle

States of matter

Planets in space

INDEX